# BERLITZ®

# COSTA DEL SOL
# and Andalusia

**1989/1990 Edition**

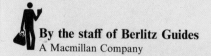

**By the staff of Berlitz Guides**
A Macmillan Company

# How to use our guide

- All the **practical information,** hints and tips that you will need before and during the trip start on page 100.
- The introduction on page 6 gives an appreciation of Andalusia and its people.
- For an overview of the region's **history,** consult the chapter A Brief History, pages 14 to 24.
- **Resorts** and **places of interest** along the coast are described between pages 25 and 56, while **destinations inland** are featured between pages 56 and 76.
- Our own choice of sights most highly recommended is pinpointed by the Berlitz traveller symbol.
- Details about **sports** and **shopping** are given in the section What to Do, beginning on page 76.
- **Entertainment** possibilities, including information on flamenco and the bullfight, figure between pages 85 and 90.
- **Restaurants, food, wine** and **spirits** are the subject of the chapter beginning on page 92.
- Finally, there is an **index** at the back of the book, pages 127–128.

---

*Although we make every effort to ensure the accuracy of all the information in this book, changes occur incessantly. We cannot therefore take responsibility for facts, prices, addresses and circumstances in general that are constantly subject to alteration. Our guides are updated on a regular basis as we reprint, and we are always grateful to readers who let us know of any errors, changes or serious omissions they come across.*

Text: Earleen Brunner
Photography: Ken Welsh
Layout: Doris Haldemann
We are particularly grateful to Harriet Brunner for her help in the preparation of this book. We also wish to thank Mark Little of Lookout Magazine in Fuengirola for his valuable advice and assistance. We appreciate, too, the considerable contribution of the Spanish National Tourist Office, especially the Geneva office.
Cartography: Falk-Verlag, Hamburg.

# Contents

# The Region and the People

Spain's sun coast is brash, booming—and still building at a frantic rate. From Almería to Tarifa, a fabulous sprawl of resort hotels, holiday villages, *urbanizaciones* and time-share developments lines the 382-kilometre (238-mi) coastal strip. Everyone wants a piece of the action, a place in the sun. And sun there is in plenty, 330 days a year. No wonder the Costa del Sol is one of Europe's favoured tourist destinations, the preferred holiday spot of some 4 million visitors every year.

Protected by a screen of mountains—the Sierra Nevada stretches east of Málaga, the Serranía de Ronda lies to the west—the coast suffers none of the climatic extremes of inland Andalusia. Even in the depths of winter, the thermometer averages an equable 16 °C

(60 °F), while sea breezes moderate summer's highs of 30 °C (86 °F) and more.

A coastal highway, the N 340, travels between the mountains and the sea, linking the widespread resort centres to the port city of Málaga, kingpin of the Costa del Sol. On the easternmost stretch, around Adra and Motril, the road thrusts through rich agricultural land, planted variously with avocado, citrus and custard-apple trees, sugar cane, bananas and bamboo. Here and there, a crane stands silhouetted against the sky, an intimation of large-scale development to come, while the occasional Moorish tower recalls age-old conflicts.

Beyond the expanding resort of Salobreña, the road climbs through rugged hills to form a spectacular corniche. Look down and you see small coves

*Dockside, Puerto Banús: the Costa del Sol is all sunshine and smiles.*

and scattered beaches of sand and shingle. Look out and you survey the sweep of the Mediterranean, gleaming gold to a far horizon.

Tourist installations and white stucco residential complexes proliferate around Nerja, a seaside haven for upwards of 80,000 holidaymakers in the peak summer season. But the coast really comes into its own west of Málaga, with Torremolinos, the original boomtown of the Costa del Sol. High-rise hotels and apartment blocks loom large at seafront, and there's a spate of snooker clubs, roller discos, bars and pubs.

More hotels, most of them high-rise, line the way to Fuengirola. Though some local residents call the one-time fishing village an urbanistic disaster, for the floods of tourists, package and otherwise, who holiday here, Fuengirola fulfills its promise of sun and sea.

So does exclusive Marbella, playground of the jet set. Back in the 1950s, Prince Alfonso von Hohenlohe put the town on the map. Today oil-rich Arab potentates keep it in the news. Admittedly, petrol-dollars come in handy in Marbella, whether you're playing for broke at the Nueva Andalucía Casino, or paying the bill for a night in the world's most expensive hotel suite.

Like Marbella, neighbouring Puerto Banús attracts the beautiful people. They frequent the cafés, bars and restaurants along the harbourfront, where yachts from five continents lie at anchor. What is more, Puerto Banús offers some of the most sophisticated shopping this side of St. Tropez—evenings and Sundays included.

Towards Estepona, a dwindling number of hoardings announce building plots, golf villas and pueblo apartments for sale. There are stretches of empty beach, and you can make out the hazy bulk of Gibraltar on the horizon, coupled to the thin blue line of Africa, beyond. Seen from a distance, the Rock has no substance at all. Algeciras, across the bay, affords a closer glimpse, while Tarifa, southernmost point of the Spanish peninsula, guards the entrance to the Strait.

The Moors took Gibraltar in 711, the year they launched their conquest of Spain. Christian forces finally recaptured it seven and a half centuries later. Then in 1704,

8

*The old ways linger a little longer behind the glittering coastal strip.*

the "key to the Mediterranean" fell into England's hands, and there it remains—a relic of empire and a bone of contention between Spain and Great Britain. History has been made on these shores since Phoenician traders and Roman colonists settled here—and 20th-century entrepreneurs and property developers are writing the latest chapter.

Wherever you base yourself on the Costa del Sol, you'll have access to sports facilities and instruction that are second to none. Swim, sail, windsurf, water-ski—or simply laze in the sun. Enrol in a tennis clinic or rise to the challenge of championship golf. You can even go skiing on Europe's most southerly slopes: Solynieve, northeast of Málaga in the Sierra Nevada, guarantees snow in season on runs that go up to a lofty 3,500 metres (11,000 feet).

Nearly every resort has some kind of tourist attraction to offer, from Nerja's cave (Cro-Magnon man sheltered here) to Fuengirola's small zoo. A burro "taxi" service ferries visitors around the village of Mijas, self-proclaimed *pueblo de interés turístico*. In the Torremolinos area, Aquapark lures the crowds off the beach with wave pools and water slides, and when the sun goes down, the rides, restaurants and nightclubs of Tívoli World take over.

Away from the coast, a day trip brings you to the great cities of Andalusia: Ronda, with its 18th-century bullring, where the *fiesta brava* was born; Jerez, venerable centre of the sherry trade; Sevilla, famed for

*Tourists keep in the swim at Torremolinos.*

10

its cathedral; Córdoba, one-time capital of Moorish Spain; Granada, site of the Alhambra. Tour operators in the resorts organize excursions to these historic centres, as well as outings closer to home—donkey rides, barbecues and the like.

What with all the fast-food emporia and the explosion of foreign-owned eating houses along the coast—every other expatriate seems to be a restaurateur—you could very well avoid an encounter with Spanish food. That would be a regrettable omission. For the coast forms part of Andalusia, one of the great gastronomic regions of Spain. This is the home of *gazpacho* and Serrano ham, two specialities any newcomer should try. To go with it, there's cooling *sangría*, now nearly as popular abroad as it is on Spain's southern shores. Local wines also merit investigation, from the sherries of Jerez to sweet Málaga.

Throughout the year, visitors

to the coast can participate in a full roster of festivals, pilgrimages and sundry celebrations. Málaga's Holy Week processions evoke the same religious fervour as that of Sevilla. May festivals in Estepona and Nerja feature costumed parades, fireworks, folk dancing and concerts. In July, all the seaside towns pay tribute to the Virgen del Carmen, patron saint of fishermen; regattas, processions and fireworks on the water are the order of the day. August sees a festival of music and dance in Nerja (the cave is the venue), while Málaga's fair features theatrical performances and other cultural events.

After dark, it's a lively scene on the Costa del Sol. Two gambling casinos operate from dusk till dawn, one in Benalmádena-Costa, the other in Marbella. Torremolinos boasts a remarkable concentration of bars, night clubs and discotheques—an Iberian Sunset Strip, where entertainment can be raucous, even tawdry. Nerja offers more of the same, on a somewhat smaller scale. Marbella raves it up in style at a succession of smart hotel clubs and trendy night spots. People here keep very busy on the social circuit, too. In all the resorts, flamenco spectaculars are staged for tourists, but there's no substitute for pure flamenco in the authentic Andalusian tradition. Nothing expresses so well the spirit of the people, their vitality, courage and dignity.

Like all Spaniards, Andalusians are generous and tolerant to a fault. Outnumbered by foreigners on their home territory, they take the tourist invasion in their stride, welcoming the prosperity and enhanced opportunity it has brought. Not that life in the sun doesn't have its problems. Dirty beaches, polluted seas and a rising crime rate have plagued the Costa del Sol, as other popular resort areas. However, vigorous measures have been taken to clean up the beaches, the water and the crime.

Taxi drivers, waiters, hotelkeepers—most of the people you meet are open and friendly, anxious to please. Many of them have experience of employment abroad in countries where relations between people are fairly circumscribed. They go out of their way to show visitors to the coast that Spain is different.

Sun, sea, pleasant people—no one could ask for more. Today's tourist is tomorrow's resident, and so, the boom goes on.

# Landmark Events

| | |
|---|---|
| c. 23,000 **B.C.** | Prehistoric man first inhabited caves in Southern Spain. |
| c. 3000 B.C. | Iberian tribes migrated to Spain from North Africa. |
| 1100 B.C. | Phoenicians founded coastal settlements. |
| 900 B.C. | Celts wandered south from northern Europe. |
| 650 B.C. | Greek traders founded a series of colonies. |
| 2nd century B.C. | Romans conquered Spain, incorporating Andalusia in the province of Baetica. |
| **A.D.** 5th century | Visigothic kingdom established. |
| 711 | Moors launched their conquest of Spain. |
| 929 | Caliphate of Córdoba founded. |
| 11th–12th centuries | The caliphate splintered into small kingdoms called *taifas*. Almoravid warriors moved in (1086), followed by the Almohads (1151). |
| 1212 | Christians defeated Moors at Las Navas de Tolosa. |
| 1232 | Nasrid dynasty founded in Granada. |
| 1492 | Granada fell to Ferdinand and Isabella. Christopher Columbus discovered America. |
| 16th century | Emperor Charles V and Philip II expanded Spain's empire during the Golden Age. Barbary pirates raided Costa del Sol. |
| 1609 | The *moriscos* were expelled from Spain. |
| 1704 | Great Britain captured Gibraltar. |
| 1808 | Napoleon set his brother, Joseph, on the Spanish throne, triggering the War of Independence (1808–14). |
| 1902–31 | Political unrest grew under King Alfonso XIII. |
| 1936–39 | Spanish Civil War. |
| 1939–75 | Dictatorship of General Francisco Franco. |
| 1950s | Tourist boom began on the Costa del Sol. |
| 1975 | Spain returned to democracy. Monarchy restored. |
| 1981 | King Juan Carlos helped to thwart a military coup. |
| 1986 | Spain entered European Economic Community. |

# A Brief History

Long before tourists invaded the Costa del Sol, Phoenicians, Greeks, Romans and Arabs passed this way. They came as traders, colonists, conquerors. For since time immemorial the coast has been a crossroads of the Mediterranean: gateway to the Atlantic, it also serves as a bridge between Africa and Spain.

Prehistoric man took up residence here some 25,000 years ago. A hunter and gatherer, he fashioned tools and weapons of stone and created some remarkable works of art, still visible today in the caves he inhabited: Nerja's seaside cavern and La Pileta, deep below ground in the Serranía de Ronda.

Neolithic peoples arrived on the scene beginning in the 4th millennium B.C. Early agriculturalists, they also practiced the art of pottery making. Examples of Neolithic ceramics—among the oldest known in Europe—were discovered in La Pileta Cave, which also preserves some impressive drawings of animals and men.

Tribes of Iberians from North Africa crossed into Spain around 3000 B.C. Not long afterwards the first experiments in architecture were made. Spain's oldest "building" stands in Antequera: a dolmen known popularly as Romeral Cave.

Bands of Celts entered the peninsula from northern Europe in the centuries after 900 B.C., bringing with them knowledge of metallurgy (bronze and iron). As they moved south, they merged with the Iberians to form a new tribal group. Soon Celt-Iberian walled villages sprang up along the coast.

## Traders and Colonizers

Meanwhile, Phoenicians were venturing across the Mediterranean from present-day Lebanon. They reached Spain by about 1100 B.C., founding many trading settlements in the "remote" or "hidden land" they named *Span* or *Spania*. First was Gadir (modern Cádiz), followed by Malaka (now Málaga) and Abdera (Adra) on the Costa del Sol. Contact with the Phoenicians introduced the Celt-Iberians to the concept of currency as a means of exchange.

After about 650 B.C., Greek traders entered the competition for Spain's rich mineral deposits and fertile land. The influence of Greece, never dominant on the Costa del Sol, was short-lived, although the olive and the grape, a Greek legacy, are important crops here.

The Carthaginians, a North African people related to the Phoenicians, subsequently took over much of southern Spain, beginning with Cádiz in 501 B.C. They extended their influence along the River Guadalquivir to Córdoba and Sevilla. On the Costa del Sol, they founded the city of Carteya, overlooking the Bay of Algeciras (240 B.C.). Fish processing plants were set up and trade in minerals flourished.

Carthage, challenged by Rome in the First Punic War (264–241 B.C.), lost most of its holdings in Spain through Iberian attacks. But the fortunes of Carthage changed with an initial victory in the Second Punic War (218–201 B.C.). Emboldened, the Carthaginian general Hannibal decided to advance on Rome. He led one of history's greatest military marches from Spain to Italy, crossing the Pyrenees and the Alps on the way. The Romans invaded Spain to cut off Hannibal's supply route—and stayed there 600 years.

## Roman Rule

It took the Romans two centuries to subdue the Iberians, but in the end, most of the peninsula was incorporated into the new colony of Hispania. The south formed part of the province of Baetica, virtually identical to today's Andalusia, with Córdoba for its capital.

There's no doubt that the Roman presence in Spain had a far-reaching influence on the country. A road network was constructed—the Via Augusta traversed the south coast on its way to Rome—and bridges, aqueducts, villas and public buildings went up. Stability and a certain unity were promoted by the introduction of Latin, from which modern Spanish developed; Roman law, still the basis of Spain's legal system; and eventually, Christianity.

But the Roman empire, overstretched and increasingly corrupt, began to crumble. The Romans withdrew from Spain, leaving the country to be overrun by various barbarian tribes, especially the Vandals. These tribes were eventually dominated by the Visigoths, who controlled much of southern Spain for some 300 years. Ultimately, the Visigothic kingdom proved unstable. The monarchy was elective, rather than hereditary, and in a dispute over succession to the crown, the disaffected party looked to North Africa for an ally.

## Moors and Christians

In A.D. 711, 12,000 Berber troops landed at Gibraltar, led by the Arab chief Tarik. Thus began 800 years of Moorish rule—and Christian opposition. Victorious at the battle of Guadalete, the Moors (the name given to Muslims in Spain) carried all before them. They pushed the Visigoths to the mountains of the north, and within ten years most of the country had fallen to Islam. To this day, Tarifa, Algeciras, Benalmádena, Almuñécar and many coastal towns more are known by their Arabic names. So, for that matter, is Andalusia, originally Al Andalus.

The Moors chose Córdoba as their seat of government, and from the 8th to 11th centuries it ranked as one of the great cities of the world, famed for its culture and erudition. Abd-er-Rahman I established the Umaiyyad dynasty here in 756. Thirty years later, he ordered construction of the grand mosque, still Córdoba's most impressive monument.

A metropolis of half a million people in its heyday, the city was capital of the independent caliphate of Córdoba, founded by Abd-er-Rahman III in 929. Under the caliphs, southern Spain knew prosperity and peace, for the Moors were relatively tolerant rulers and taxed non-believers rather than trying to convert them. Intellectual life flourished, and advances were made in science and medicine.

With the introduction of a sophisticated irrigation system, rice, cotton and sugar cane were cultivated for the first time on Spanish soil, as well as oranges, peaches and pomegranates. The manufacture of paper and glass was another Moorish innovation. Skilled engineers and architects, the Moors built numerous palaces and fortifications. Superb craftsmen, they excelled at ceramics, tooled leather and silver work.

If the rise of Córdoba was remarkable, so was its fall. Early in the 11th century, the caliphate splintered into a number of small kingdoms called *taifas*, constantly warring among themselves. The Christians in the north, seeing the enemy weaken, captured the *taifa* of Toledo. Under threat of attack, the other *taifas* sought help from the Almoravids, fanatical Berber warriors. They marched against the Christians in 1086

*Abd-er-Rahman I built for the ages. His 8th-century fortress is Almería's oldest landmark.*

and went on to reduce Moorish Spain to a province of their own North African empire. For a time, the affairs of Muslim Spain were administered in Granada—until the Almoravids lost their grip on the peninsula, succumbing to the luxuries of life in Andalusia.

The pattern repeated itself a century later when the Moors invoked the aid of the Almohads in 1151. These primitive tribesmen from the Atlas mountains soon made them-

*King Ferdinand and Queen Isabella ride to victory over the Moors.*

selves the masters of southern Spain. They constructed fortifications like Sevilla's Alcázar, endowing the Moors with enough strength to resist the Christian forces a while longer.

Fortunes swayed to and fro until 1212, when the Christians gained their first decisive victory at Las Navas de Tolosa in northern Andalusia. The Christians gradually captured and annexed former bastions of Moorish rule: in 1236 Córdoba fell to James the Conqueror, followed by Sevilla in 1248. The Moors were on the retreat, retrenching along the coast and withdrawing to the strongholds of Ronda and Granada.

In military disarray and political decline, Moorish Spain nevertheless saw another two centuries of brilliance under the Nasrid dynasty, founded in Granada by Mohammed I in 1232. Refugees from Córdoba and Sevilla flooded into the city, bringing with them their talents and skills. The palace of the Alhambra was constructed as a setting for a luxurious court life dedicated to the pursuit of literature, music and the arts.

Now on the front line, the fortresses along the coast came under attack. Sancho IV took Gibraltar in 1310, but the Christians later relinquished

**For the Greater Good**

After the capture of Tarifa, Sancho IV entrusted the defence of the city to one Alonso Pérez de Guzmán, known as Guzmán the Good. Guzmán held Tarifa at immense personal cost, for his young son, a page in the service of Sancho, fell into the hands of the infidel.

Given the ultimatum of surrender or the murder of the boy, Guzmán threw down a dagger from the citadel and kept to his post, choosing "honour without a son, to a son with dishonour".

their prize, held by the Moors until 1462. Then, in the 1480s, the Christians launched a new offensive: Ronda capitulated to Ferdinand and Isabella in 1485, followed by Málaga in 1487 and Almería in 1488. All Christendom gave thanks when Granada was conquered at last in 1492. That same year, Christopher Columbus discovered America in the name of the Spanish crown. A new era had begun.

**Golden Age**

With the triumph of Christianity, the country was united under the "Catholic Monarchs", a title conferred by Pope Alexander VI on Ferdinand II of Aragon and Isabella I **19** of Castile. Fanatical in their religious zeal, the king and queen expelled from Spain all Jews who refused to convert to Christianity (1492), followed by the Moors in 1502. In so doing, they reneged on their promise of religious freedom, made on the fall of Granada. With the Jews who left Spain went many of the country's bankers and merchants, and with the Moors, a good number of its agriculturalists and labourers.

For their part, converted Jews (conversos) and Moors (moriscos) were viewed with suspicion by the Inquisition, established by the Catholic Monarchs to stamp out heresy. Many conversos and moriscos fled the country or were condemned to death.

The 16th century was glorious for Spain. The conquest of the New World brought Spain prestige and wealth. Sevilla, port for the Americas, had a monopoly on trade with Spain's territories there, granted by Queen Isabella. For over two centuries, no city in the country was richer.

By comparison, the Costa del Sol languished, subject to raids by Barbary pirates. The king ordered construction of watch towers along the coast, but he was powerless to stop Barbary attacks. Under constant threat for more than 200 years, the population concentrated inland, in towns and villages hidden in the foothills of the sierra. Rumour had it that the moriscos passed intelligence to the pirates. People also suspected them of abetting the Turks, the rising power in the Mediterranean.

As Emperor Charles V of the Holy Roman Empire, the king turned his attention to events in Europe. Between 1521 and 1556, he went to war with France four times, squandering the riches of the Americas on ceaseless campaigns. Charles also had a weakness for costly architectural projects like the vast Renaissance palace in the grounds of the Alhambra, which he commissioned in 1526. Morisco tax money financed construction, abandoned for lack of funds when the moriscos revolted 12 years into the reign of Philip II (1556–1598). The king dispatched his half-brother, Don Juan of Austria, to quell the rebellion, which ended in 1570 with the defeat of the moriscos and their dispersal throughout Spain*.

*The unfortunate affair didn't end there. In 1609 the moriscos were expelled from Spain by order of Philip III, with serious consequences for the country's agricultural productivity.

The rout of the Turkish fleet at Lepanto the following year left Spain in control of the Mediterranean, but dominance was short-lived. In 1588 Philip II made ready to invade England, only to be repulsed at the outset when the English navy destroyed Spain's Invincible Armada. The battle marked the start of slow decline for Spain

Philip's military adventures and his taste for grandiose architecture left Spain encumbered with debts. Participation in the Thirty Years' War under Philip III led to further financial difficulties and another debacle. Spanish troops were defeated by the French at Rocroi in Flanders (1643), never to regain their former prestige.

## French Ascendancy

Spain's internal affairs became the concern of other great powers after Charles II died without heirs. The Archduke Charles of Austria rivalled France's Philip of Bourbon, designated to ascend the throne, in the ensuing War of the Spanish Succession. On the Costa del Sol, Gibraltar was the scene of fierce fighting in 1704, when Great Britain captured the Rock on behalf of its ally, Austria. Unable to oust the British, Spain finally was forced to relinquish claims to Gibraltar in 1713, by terms of the Treaty of Utrecht, which also confirmed Philip's right to the Spanish throne.

Nearly a hundred years later, during the Napoleonic wars, Spanish ships fought alongside the French fleet against Lord Nelson at Cape Trafalgar, south-east of Cádiz. But as the wars continued, Napoleon, distrustful of his ally, forced the Spanish king, Ferdinand VII, to abdicate in 1808 and imposed his brother, Joseph, as king. He sent thousands of troops across the Pyrenees to subjugate the Spaniards, who then revolted.

Aided by British troops subsequently commanded by the Duke of Wellington, they drove the French out of the Iberian peninsula. At Tarifa, the enemy was defeated literally overnight in an offensive of 1811. What the world knows as the Peninsular War (1808–14) is referred to in Spain as the War of Independence. During this period, the country's first, though short-lived, constitution was drafted and the colonies of South America won independence.

## Troubled Times

Ferdinand's return to the throne in 1814 destroyed hopes for a constitutional monarchy, while tension between liberals and conservatives led to a century of conflict, marked by the upheavals of the three Carlist wars and the abortive First Republic, proclaimed in 1873.

For the Costa del Sol, the 19th century was a time of tentative expansion. With piracy at an end, towns and villages grew up along the shoreline. And the extension of the railway to Almería in 1899 promoted the early development of the eastern area.

Alfonso XIII, a young man of only 16, took up his duties as king in 1902. His reign was a difficult time for Spain. Prosperity and stability eluded the country, which remained neutral during World War I.

Against a background of violence, strikes and regional strife, the king accepted the dictatorship of General Miguel Primo de Rivera in 1923. Seven years later, the opposition of radical forces toppled Primo de Rivera from power. Neither reform nor the maintenance of order seemed possible. The king went into exile following anti-royalist election results in 1931, and another republic was founded.

The 1933 parliamentary elections resulted in a swing to the right, as public opinion polarized. When the left came out on top in the elections of 1936, the situation deteriorated rapidly. Six months later, General Francisco Franco led a large section of the army in revolt against the government.

Support for the Nationalist rising came from monarchists and conservatives, as well as the right-wing Falangist organization and the Roman Catholic Church, while liberals, socialists, communists and anarchists cast their lot with the government. Early on, the conflict assumed an international character, involving Germany and Italy on the Nationalist side, with Russia and the volunteers of the International Brigade for the Republicans.

The bloodshed lasted three years and cost hundreds of thousands of lives. General Franco emerged as leader of a shattered Spain. Many Republicans went into exile; others simply disappeared. The Republican mayor of Mijas caused a sensation when he finally surfaced in the 1960s after three decades in hiding, in his own home.

Franco kept Spain out of World War II, despite Hitler's entreaties to the contrary. Nor did Gibraltar participate actively in the conflict. Slowly the Spanish nation healed its wounds, though conditions in the country were difficult and life was hard.

## On the Up and Up

All that changed, virtually overnight, as Spain's tourist potential began to be exploited in the 1950s. The government made credit available for the development of hotels and apartment blocks in coastal areas, including the Costa del Sol. Soon fishing villages like

*Man for our times, King Juan Carlos dominates the Spanish scene.*

Torremolinos and Marbella sprouted suburbs, and the boom was on, gaining momentum with Spain's admission to the United Nations in **23**

1955. The advent of jet and package travel in the 1960s opened the coast to mass tourism, with profound consequences for the economy and the people.

On the death of General Franco in 1975, Spain returned to democracy. In accordance with Franco's wishes, the monarchy was restored in the person of King Juan Carlos, grandson of the Bourbon Alfonso XIII. No mere figurehead, the king helped thwart a military coup in 1981, keeping Spain firmly on a democratic course.

Nowadays, the country boasts one of Europe's progressive governments, committed to Spain's successful integration into the European Economic Community. As a precondition to admission, the border to Gibraltar was opened in February 1985, after a 16-year hiatus. However, the issue of sovereignty, long at a stalemate, remains to be negotiated. That Great Britain should possess this piece of Spanish soil irks Spaniards. For their part, the British are loath to relinquish their long-time colony.

Come what may, the future of the Costa del Sol itself looks secure. For Spaniards as for foreigners, the good life is here.

**Finding Your Way**

| | |
|---|---|
| alcazaba | fortress |
| alcázar | castle citadel |
| ascensor | lift, elevator |
| autopista | motorway, highway |
| avenida | avenue |
| ayuntamiento | town hall |
| barrio | quarter |
| cabo | cape |
| calle | street |
| carretera | road |
| castillo | castle |
| ciudad vieja | old town |
| correos | post office |
| cueva | cave |
| estación de ferrocarril | railway station |
| faro | lighthouse |
| fortaleza | fortress |
| iglesia | church |
| isla | island |
| jardín | garden |
| mercado | market |
| mezquita | mosque |
| muelle | docks |
| murallas | ramparts |
| museo | museum |
| oficina de turismo | tourist office |
| paseo | boulevard |
| playa | beach |
| plaza | square |
| plaza de toros | bullring |
| puerto | harbour |
| río | river |
| sierra | mountain range |
| vía | avenue |
| derecha | right |
| izquierda | left |
| todo derecho | straight ahead |

# Where to Go

Most visitors to the Costa del Sol base themselves in one of the large seaside resorts—Nerja, Torremolinos, Fuengirola, Marbella—travelling from there to the other coastal towns, with an obligatory stop in Gibraltar and a side trip or two up into the mountains. Some people go farther afield, to Sevilla, Córdoba and Granada. Tour operators offer popular one-day coach excursions, but driving

*The Costa del Sol wins the resort sweepstakes hands down.*

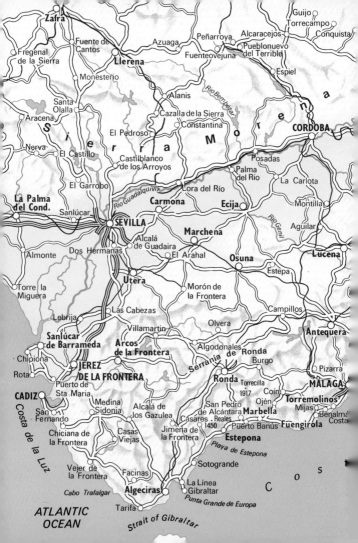

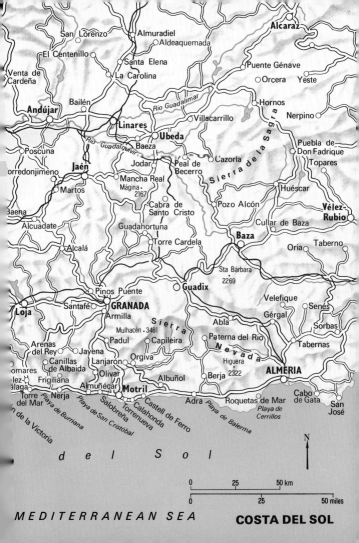

**COSTA DEL SOL**

yourself there and back really isn't practicable in a day. To get the most out of a visit, stay overnight—or hire a helicopter.

We begin our tour of the coast in the gateway city of Málaga, site of the international airport and main seaport of entry. After a look at the major monuments and museums, we head west along the N 340 to Torremolinos, Benalmádena and Fuengirola, and up into the hills to Mijas and Alhaurín el Grande. Back on the coast, we continue to exclusive Marbella and surroundings: Puerto Banús, Nueva Andalucía and San Pedro de Alcántara seaside; Ojén and Monda inland. Then it's on to Algeciras and Tarifa via Estepona, San Roque, La Línea and neighbouring Gibraltar. East of Málaga, we make for Nerja, carrying on from there to Almuñécar and Salobreña. Past Motril and Adra comes journey's end, the cathedral city of Almería, at the eastern limit of the coast.

# Málaga

For tourists from beach resorts up and down the coast, Málaga offers a taste of the real Spain. There are twisting, narrow streets, cool public gardens, an old Moorish fortress and waterfront promenade—with plenty of traditional bar and café life and bullfights on Sunday.

The city looks back on more than 3,000 years of history. Founded by Phoenician traders, it came under Cartha-ginian, and then Roman, rule. Next on the scene were the Visigoths, who destroyed most of the ancient town. The Moors fortified Málaga when they moved in in 711, building the settlement into a major port. A Moorish stronghold for centuries, Málaga fell at last to Christian forces in 1487. It took 60,000 men and a siege of 3½ months to force a surrender.

Set at the foot of the Gibralfaro—the hill that is Málaga's trademark—the city sprawls between the sierra and the sea. With a population of half a million, it's fairly extensive, though nearly everything of interest to tourists lies within the cross-hatch of streets in the old quarter. A good way to visit the capital of the Costa del Sol is on one of the bus excursions organized in the various resort centres. It takes real stamina to trek round the city in the heat of summer—and to cope with the chaotic traffic any time of the year. Winter and summer, Málaga slumbers through the siesta hour—1.30 to 4 (winter) or 5 p.m—so plan to do your

*Big city in the sun, Malaga is undisputed capital of the coast. Tower blocks overlook the old bullring and the expanding port.* **29**

sightseeing and shopping in the morning or late afternoon.

City tours take in the cathedral, bullring and Gibralfaro area, with a stop at a *bodega*, or wine cellar, to sample Málaga's famous sweet red wine. If you can find time for a return visit, don't miss the fascinating folk art museum, housed in an old inn, and the Museum of Fine Arts, with paintings from the childhood of Picasso.

## City Sights

A good place to begin a tour of Málaga is at the top—some 425 feet (130 m) above the city on the summit of pine-clad **Gibralfaro** (Lighthouse Hill)*.

Stop first at the state-run *parador,* a historic hostelry in a spectacular situation, for a superb view of Málaga and its surroundings—from the bullring just below you, to the port and *paseo,* to the sandy sweep of Málaga beach. On a clear day—and that means just about every day hereabouts—you can see all the way to Fuengirola, a distance of 30 kilometres (18 mi).

Another footpath links the

---

* A footpath leads uphill from Paseo del Parque, but tourists who follow this route may be a target for pickpockets or thieves. To be on the safe side, go by taxi or in your own car.

*parador* to the rambling ruins of a Phoenician castle reconstructed in the 14th century by the Moors, who went on to build the lighthouse which gave Gibralfaro its name. Again, it's advisable to drive up to the ramparts, which enclose gardens open to the public all day long. The site is a lonely one, best visited with a tour group or a large party.

On your way back into town you may want to take a closer look at Málaga's **bullring** *(plaza de toros)*, a colonnaded 19th-century construction. On Sundays, capacity crowds of 14,000 gather to watch the heirs of Joselito and Manolete in the arena. A small museum on the premises recalls some thrilling moments in the history of the *corrida.*

Created on reclaimed land, the **Paseo del Parque** parallels the waterfront. Palm and plane trees, bougainvillea, aloes and geraniums luxuriate in this tropical garden by the sea. Midway along the avenue, past the town hall and post office, Plaza de la Aduana gives on to the **Alcazaba,** the sprawling Moorish fortress that made Málaga a stronghold of Al Andalus. Across from the entrance lie the partially excavated ruins of a Roman theatre, the only visible remains of the ancient city.

MÁLAGA

## Getting Around

Driving on the coast can be difficult in the high season, owing to the sheer number of tourists on the road. There's just one east-west route, the N 340, which travels through the centre of a number of resorts. Congestion, numerous pedestrians, frequent traffic lights, some sharp curves and the absence of bypasses or roundabouts (traffic circles) at major intersections make this motorway one of Europe's most dangerous.

So it's only sensible to take the following precautions:

● Avoid left turns, except at traffic lights or roundabouts.

● Signal if you have to stop behind a car turning left: the left-turn lane also serves as the fast lane for through traffic.

● Keep plenty of distance between your vehicle and the one ahead of you.

● Don't exceed posted speed limits, slowing down where indicated on curves and in towns.

● Be on the look-out for cars entering and exiting the motorway: there are few acceleration and deceleration lanes.

● Take care when overtaking (passing). Lorry (truck) drivers often signal when the way is clear.

● Don't drink and drive.

It's a bit of a climb up the hillside to the portal dubbed Puerta del Cristo (Gateway of Christ). Victorious Christian troops under Ferdinand and Isabella celebrated mass here when the fortress finally fell into their hands in 1487. Higher still, the one-time palace of the Moors contains a modest museum of classical and Islamic artefacts, including fragments of Roman statues and Hispano-Moresque pottery.

Only partially restored, the royal precinct proves a letdown for anyone who expects a little Alhambra. But the view doesn't disappoint: like Málaga's Moorish kings, you look down on a breathtaking panorama of sky and sea, with the city at your feet.

Paseo del Parque comes to an end at **Plaza de la Marina**, with its playing fountains and statue of that popular character of old Málaga, *El Cenachero,* the itinerant fish vendor, carrying his panniers of sardines and anchovies.

Calle de Molina Lario runs from the square to the **Cathedral**, known as the "little lady with one arm" because it remains unfinished: one huge tower reaches 330 feet (100 m) upwards, but work on the other, a forlorn stump of stone, stopped in 1783. Under construction for three centuries, the Renaissance building incorporates Baroque and Neoclassical elements.

Students of art the world over know Málaga as the birthplace of Pablo Picasso, who left his native city at age 14 for the more cosmopolitan climate of Madrid and Barcelona. The **Museo de Bellas Artes** (Fine Arts Museum), around the corner from the cathedral in Calle de San Agustín, preserves some of the furniture from the Picasso family home (still standing at Plaza de la Merced 6), as well as works by the young Picasso and his first teacher, Antonio Muñoz Degrain. The precocious *Los Viejos* (The Old Couple), produced at the age of ten under Muñoz's tutelage, already shows signs of genius. Apart from the Picassos, the museum displays paintings and sculpture by Luís de Morales, Murillo (notice the spiritual *Saint Francis of Paul*), Alonso Cano (an intense *Saint John the Evangelist* stands out) and Pedro de Mena, with special emphasis on the masters of the 19th-century Málaga school. Recently renovated, the building itself is of interest. This old palace in Renaissance style encloses pleasant courtyards abloom with flowers.

A city of commerce as well as culture, Málaga offers shopping of a traditional nature along three main thoroughfares: Molina Lario, Calle de Marqués de Larios (completely rebuilt after the Civil War), and the pedestrian Calle de Granada. You can buy almost anything here, from foodstuffs to footwear. This is also the place to sample Málaga's sweet red wines, the speciality of the house in bars and *tabernas* throughout the neighbourhood.

People who live in the historic centre of Málaga shop daily for food in the century-old **Mercado Central**. You enter the market through a horseshoe-shaped gateway that is a relic of the Moorish city walls. Though the ramparts of brick are gone, the bazaar atmosphere of the *zoco* (the marketplace of the Moors) lives on, as fishmongers, butchers, greengrocers and spice sellers all vie for customers. They display the bounty of Málaga province: pyramids of oranges and almonds, heaps of swordfish and shellfish, braids of garlic, strings of sausage and the most fragrant bouquets of wild thyme.

The **Museo de Artes Populares** is a charming little folk art museum installed in a historic inn of 1632, the Posada de la Victoria. It lies at the western boundary of the old quarter, beside the Guadalmedina, Málaga's sluggish river. Exhibits take you back to that time before the boom when the tourist resorts were small fishing villages and people lived from the sea. Retired from use not so very long ago, an old forge and a bakery with millstone and wood-burning oven, a *bodega* (wine cellar) and printer's workshop all make fascinating tableaux. There's an array of popular ceramics on display and some appealing rustic furniture (notice the well-used birth chair).

## Environs of Málaga

Follow the course of the Guadalmedina north 7 kilometres (4 mi) to **Finca de la Concepción**, an estate surrounded by beautiful gardens. Weekdays the public is admitted to the grounds, an oasis of green in an arid landscape of crumpled hills. Enhancing the scenic attractions are Roman remains from Málaga and Cártama (classical Cartima).

Closer to town, restaurants on the beaches of Pedregalejo and El Palo serve the freshest seafood around. Take a seat by the sea and tuck into a heaped plateful of *fritura malagueña,* the deep-fried catch of the day.

# West to Tarifa

Some of the most popular beach resorts in the world line the 100-mile (162-km) stretch of coast between Málaga and Tarifa on the Strait of Gibraltar. If it's action you're after, you'll enjoy the swinging scene of Torremolinos, Fuengirola and Marbella. The centres further west are quieter, more family orientated, with the emphasis on sports and beach life, rather than night-time revels.

## Torremolinos

First comes Torremolinos (13 km/8 mi), fun capital of the Costa del Sol, offering everything a sun-hungry holidaymaker could wish for in the way of beaches, bars, pubs, restaurants, nightclubs and discotheques—not to mention human contact of every shape, language and description.

Centre of it all is Plaza Costa del Sol and the contiguous **Calle San Miguel**, with its much-photographed profusion of shop signs. At the bottom of San Miguel, a flight of steps leads down towards a 6-mile (10 km) sweep of uninterrupted beach, broken only by the rocky promontory of Castillo de Santa Clara, which separates the Bajondillo and Carihuela sections of town. A dozen or more *merendcros*—simple eating houses that serve as impromptu beach clubs—overlook the Bajondillo sea front, chock-a-block with basking bodies.

But the most lively beach restaurants are over in the "Spanish" suburb of **La Carihuela**, a former fishing village that provided James Michener with a setting for scenes in *The Drifters*. There are actually still a few bona fide fishermen about: struggle out of bed between 6 and 8 in the morning and you'll see them returning to shore in gaily painted wooden barques, hauling sardines and anchovies by the net full. For local colour of another kind, you can stay at a Scandinavian hostel, eat at a Dutch restaurant, drink at an English pub. It may not be Spain, but it's no less fun for that.

*There's talk, laughter, more talk when Spaniards get together.*

The Wax Museum *(Museo de Cera)* near the railway station is good for a half-hour's breather from the beach. While you're at it, take in the multivision show on Torremolinos past and present, screened in an auditorium on the premises. Other attractions lie close at **36** hand: the water slides of **Atlantis Aquapark** (see p. 85) and the 18-hole greens of the Parador del Golf. But the biggest draw in Torremolinos is the concentration of bars, discos and boîtes in and around Avenida Carlota Alexandra that has made the resort an international byword for non-stop nightlife.

ranks high in the tourist sweepstakes. Scattered among the hotels and blocks of holiday flats are three Moorish watch towers which stand beside the sea like outsize chess pieces. Extensive Roman ruins, still under excavation, lie to the east of one of them—Torre Quebrada.

Well endowed with bars, discos and clubs, though less frenetic by night than Torremolinos, Benalmádena-Costa also has a cultural side. Concerts and exhibitions take place in the Neo-Moresque Castillo El Bil-Bil, built by a Frenchwoman in the 1930s. The coastal highway goes right by this highly visible raspberry pink pile, topped with a crenellated tower. Inquire about activities and events in the local tourist office, installed in the gatehouse.

## Benalmádena Area

The tourist installations of Torremolinos merge seamlessly into those of neighbouring **Benalmádena-Costa**. With one of the two gambling casinos on the coast—Casino Torrequebrada, right on the N 340—and golden sands that stretch for 5½ miles (9 km), the resort

As you drive along, watch for the turn-off that leads inland a couple of kilometres (about 1 mile) to BENALMÁDENA-PUEBLO, a pleasant perched village with its own small bullring and whitewashed church. A mirador overlooks terraced hillsides that slope steeply down to the teeming coastal strip.

**37**

Benalmádena has an institution of national importance in its **Museo Arqueológico Municipal**. Some exhibits come from the locality: the Neolithic weapons, tools and ceramics were unearthed in caves around Benalmádena, while the Roman artefacts were discovered near the sea front and in offshore waters. But the museum gives pride of place to a collection of Precolumbian art (largely Mexican and Nicaraguan) said to be the most important of its kind in Spain, with jewellery, statuary and ceramics from all the major cultures and periods.

Also in the Benalmádena area, the **Tívoli World** amusement park has put the suburb of ARROYO DE LA MIEL on the tourist map (see p. 85).

*Basking on the Benalmádena beachfront (below). Local fishermen have it all sewn up.*

## Fuengirola

Nine kilometres (5½ mi) down the line, Fuengirola provides British sun-seekers with all the home pleasures. Games of darts and snooker go on all day, and beer flows like water in hundreds of public houses —more per square mile than the city of London, they say—but who's counting? Fuengirola is somewhat more subdued than Torremolinos, though far from staid, and a holiday here comes a little cheaper than in Torremolinos or Marbella. Ever expanding, the resort now incorporates the beach communities of CARVAJAL and LOS BOLICHES on its eastern flank.

Mass tourism is a fact of life for Fuengirola, full up in the high season. A second generation of hotel towers and apartment blocks fronts the **Paseo Marítimo**, a medley of concrete and glass. The **Castillo de Sohail** on the western outskirts rises above it all.

*The housewives of Andalusia air their clean linen.*

Abd-er-Rahman III built the hilltop fortress in the 10th century. Gradually a settlement grew up around the walls. Taken by the Christians in a bloody battle of 1487, Sohail was levelled on the orders of the Catholic Kings. Rebuilt, it was occupied by French troops in the Peninsular War, who left a souvenir of their stay behind them—the cannon displayed down on the *paseo*.

Town fathers run the **Zoo Municipal**, near the centre in Camino de Santiago. This eclectic collection of lions, emus, gibbons, zebras and other species was started by a local animal lover some years back.

Against all odds, a few vestiges of village life survive in Fuengirola: the commercial fishing fleet is still a going concern, and the Tuesday morning

rounded by modern villas and *urbanizaciones,* the core of the village preserves steep streets of whitewashed houses, harbouring bars, restaurants and shops, shops, shops... Traffic is banned from the centre, served by *burro* "taxis"—caparisoned beasts of burden "parked" at a rank by the **mirador**. The view from the look-out is sublime: stubbled hills slide down to an azure sea, whipped into white wavelets by the wind.

To one side of this natural balcony, a **chapel** dedicated to the Virgen de la Peña (Our Lady of the Mountain) occupies a grotto carved from living rock.

Inevitably, a visit to Mijas involves a quick round of the best stocked souvenir shops on the coast, overflowing with woven goods, esparto grass products, tooled leather and ceramic articles of all kinds. A popular holiday resort, Mijas boasts luxury hotels, luxuriant golf greens, an offbeat museum of miniature works of art *(Museo de Miniaturas)* and Spain's only square **bullring**. Said to be the oldest in the country, it dates back to Moorish times.

A panoramic if hair-raising road leads on through the Sierra de Mijas to ALHAURÍN EL GRANDE, an untidy little town that straggles out from a kernel

market *(mercadillo)* continues. Tour operators all along the coast feature a weekly excursion to the Fuengirola market, combined with a visit to the village of Mijas, 8 kilometres (5 mi) inland along the *ruta verde* (green route).

**Inland from Fuengirola**

It's not typical, but don't let that keep you away from **Mijas**. The tourist trappings are but a façade for the Andalusian soul and spirit of the place. Sur-

of white houses. Alhaurín's history is as old as the hills: its church rests on Moorish foundations, and a ruined Roman aqueduct and reservoirs still stand in the municipality.

There's no point in continuing further, unless you'd prefer to approach Marbella by the inland route. The road runs monotonously through bare, rocky hills to the market town of COÍN, descending to the coast via MONDA and OJÉN (see p. 46).

## ♣ Marbella

The aristocrat of Costa del Sol resorts, Marbella caters to the rich and titled, to royalty, celebrities and heads of state. Prices are accordingly higher here than in any other coastal town. But you get what you pay for: superior standards of accommodation, service and cuisine—as well as a superb array of recreational facilities and some of the most sophisticated shops in Spain—make Marbella the choice of discriminating holidaymakers the world over.

It's only appropriate that a queen should have given the town its name. When she first saw the coast here, Isabella of Castile is said to have exclaimed, *¡Qué mar tan bella!* (What a beautiful sea!). The Phoenicians had called their

settlement a more prosaic Salduba (Salt City).

Marbella encompasses 17 miles (28 km) of beach front, built with exclusive hotel complexes like Los Monteros, Puente Romano and the resort's original hostelry, the Marbella Club. Put up in the 1950s by Prince Alfonso von Hohenlohe, the hotel launched Marbella as a jet-set gathering place.

Guided tours of Marbella and nearby Puerto Banús are available from Málaga, Torremolinos and Fuengirola—a boon for sightseers without a car. Approaching the Marbella area from the east, you pass the *urbanizaciones* of ELVÍRIA, LAS CHAPAS and LAS LOMAS—luxury compounds that have been developed with style. The congested coastal highway plunges on through the centre of modern Marbella, taken up with sidewalk cafés, smart boutiques and estate agents' offices.

Marbella turns its most attractive face to the sea. Down by the water, a promenade swings past the urban beaches of El Fuerte and Fontanilla, and a **marina** *(Puerto Deportivo)* with anchorage for several

*Narrow streets protect you from the glare in Marbella's old town.*

hundred pleasure craft. Some lively beach bars and restaurants make this a popular part of town.

North of the main road, the **old town** provides another focus for resort life. Here in the leafy **Plaza de los Naranjos** (Square of the Orange Trees) you can nurse a coffee for hours while you admire the noble 16th-century façade of the Town Hall *(Casa Consistorial)*. Small shops are scattered through the warren of tiny, twisting streets all around. As you explore the neighbourhood, you'll come across the historic parish church and the convents of La Trinidad

*Playboys of the western world live it up in Marbella.*

and San Francisco (Cervantes, author of *Don Quixote,* lodged at the latter, they say). From Moorish times comes the storybook **castillo,** while the Romans built the bridge *(puente romano)* that spans the Río Nagüelles—in the grounds of the de luxe Hotel Puente Romano.

Monuments of the new Marbella cling to the hills on the western outskirts. You can't miss the residence of the king of Saudi Arabia: modelled after the American White House (only slightly larger), it occupies **45** a pine- and palm-covered site just above the motorway, within hailing distance of a galaxy of princely palaces. On a neighbouring rise stands Marbella's modernistic **mosque** *(Mezquita del Rey Abdulaziz Al Saud)*, open to the public every afternoon except Friday. Non-Muslims of both sexes are admitted to the serene, green-carpeted interior.

The playground of the petrol princes lies just down the road in the chic suburb of NUEVA ANDALUCÍA, one of the first purpose-built resort communities on the coast. Its magnificent harbour, **Puerto Banús**, is the St. Tropez of Spain. A thousand yachts lie at anchor, and there's a glamorous line-up of restaurants, boîtes and shops—open nights, weekends and holidays in the high season. And the wheel of fortune never stops turning at the Nueva Andalucía Casino, the place to make a king's ransom—or lose one.

Also within the orbit of Marbella, quiet SAN PEDRO DE ALCÁNTARA preserves ruins of the Roman colony of Silniana, destroyed by earthquake in the 4th century A.D. Some fine mosaic pavements have been uncovered north of town, and remains of an early Christian basilica lie south of the motorway in VEGA DEL MAR.

## Inland from Marbella

Heading due north of Marbella, you see the high peaks of the Sierra Blanca outlined against the blue, blue sky. Follow the road to the village of OJÉN (famous for its *aguardiente,* a kind of spirit) and on to the mountain pass called Puerto de Ojén. Just beyond, a turn-off leads to the **Refúgio de Juanar**, a hunting lodge in the heart of a national game preserve. This is the haunt of wild rabbit, partridge and the ibex or *capra hispanica,* unique to Spain. People come from round the world to observe, photograph and stalk this rare species of wild mountain goat.

The Juanar lodge makes an ideal base for excursions to points of interest in the Sierra Blanca. One-time domain of the marquesses of Larios, it's owned and operated as a co-operative venture by villagers of Ojén, who can arrange for guides, mounts and hunting permits with advance notice. Write direct to the Refúgio de Juanar Ojén (Málaga), Spain.

Continuing north, the road travels through a landscape of pines to MONDA, said to have been the site of a battle between Julius Caesar and his rival, Pompey. If you have the time, drive into the village and take a look around.

## Towards Tarifa

The last major resort centre on the western flank of the coast, **Estepona** provides all the essentials—beaches, golf courses, marina—in an engaging small-town atmosphere 26 kilometres (16 mi) from the sophistication of Marbella. Low-rise blocks of flats, unpretentious restaurants and hostels overlook the palm-lined **Paseo Marítimo**, furnished with a little playground and car park. Fishermen still gather to drink in back-street bars, and there are traditional cafés where you can get *churros* and chocolate of a morning.

Of Roman origin, Estepona preserves the remains of Moorish fortifications and watch towers, an 18th-century parish church and an expressionistic bullring, a startling piece of modern architecture which is beginning to look rather the worse for wear. Estepona has another claim to fame in Costa Natura, a naturist resort on the western outskirts that is the only facility of its kind on the Costa del Sol. However, nudism hardly seems a radical option in these days of general toplessness, with nudity permitted on half a dozen public beaches along the Costa del Sol—least of all in the bland surroundings of this "pueblo" complex.

Beyond Estepona, development is sporadic: stretches of open land parallel the motorway, and you can look out over the water. One spectacular sea view follows another, with the white surf crashing and flashing on the dark sandy shore. About 6 kilometres (4 mi) out of town, a mountain road takes you up to **Casares**, increasingly a goal for day-trippers from Marbella to Tarifa. Belvedere of the Sierra Bermeja, this white village spirals up a rugged hilltop to command sweeping views of the coast and countryside. Continuing west, you pass two nuclei of luxury development: PUERTO DUQUESA, emulating the success of Puerto Banús, and SOTOGRANDE, an exclusive hotel and residential enclave.

Gibraltar looms ever larger as you approach **San Roque**, established by Spanish refugees who fled the Rock when the English captured it in 1704. Building blocks for the town were found conveniently to hand in the ruins of Roman Carteya, nearby. Consequently, little remains of the classical site. To the south lies the border town of LA LÍNEA DE LA CONCEPCIÓN, experiencing a mini-boom since restrictions on travel to Gibraltar were lifted in 1985 (see p. 49).

ALGECIRAS, across the bay from Gibraltar, offers unsurpassed views of the coast's dominant geographical feature. From the harbour, hydrofoils and ferries cross the Strait to Ceuta, a Spanish possession, and to Tangier in Morocco. Popular day excursions to Ceuta and Tangier* via Algeciras depart from the major resort centres.

The Costa del Sol comes to an end at **Tarifa**, where Mediterranean and Atlantic, Europe and Africa come together. The

---

*For information on sights, food and shopping in Tangier, consult the Berlitz travel guide to MOROCCO.

Rif Mountains hang on the horizon like a spectre: Morocco is a mere 13 kilometres (8 mi) away.

In 711, the Berber warrior Tarif-ibn-Malik captured Tarifa for Islam, giving it his name. A section of the old Moorish walls still stand, along with the 10th-century fortress. Secured by Christian forces in 1292, it's now known as the **Castillo de Guzmán el Bueno**, after Alonso Pérez de Guzmán, who sacrificed the life of his own son rather than surrender to the infidel (see p. 19). Now occupied by Spain's military, the castle is open to tourists at weekends only.

# Gibraltar

The climate is a decided improvement over the fog and rain of England. And the people are largely of Mediterranean stock. But in other important respects, "Gib", as residents call Britain's long-time colony, is a perfect clone of the home country. Tea rooms, pubs and helmeted bobbies are all features of life on the Rock.

Linked to La Línea on the Spanish mainland by a narrow isthmus, this barren limestone peak soars to a height of 1,396 feet (426 m). One of the Pillars of Hercules, it was raised by the god from the seabed—or so the ancients thought—marking the limits of the known world. The name "Gibraltar" is a corruption of *Gibel-Tarik*, Rock of Tarik, the Arab chief who used Gibraltar as a bridgehead for his conquest of Spain in A.D. 711.

Some 30,000 Gibraltarians squeeze into an area of only 2½ square miles (6 sq km). The town of Gibraltar lies on the gently sloping western side of the Rock, across from Algeciras, while the village of Catalan Bay is situated at the foot of the sheer eastern face. Now that land access has been restored, a day trip to Gibraltar is perfectly feasible. You can do the rounds of the important sights in a couple of hours, leaving plenty of time for duty-free shopping (savings are slight) and gambling (round the clock) at the colony's casino.

Most tours of Gibraltar take in the ruins of the Moorish castle, the panorama from the lighthouse at Europa Point, which projects into the Bay of Algeciras, and historic Trafalgar Cemetery. Here lie the dead of the Battle of Trafalgar (1805), in which Lord Nelson lost his life. The admiral's body was brought to Gibraltar and pickled in a cask of rum so that it could be returned to England for a hero's burial.

But the highlight of a visit to Gibraltar is the cable car ride from Grand Parade to the top of the Rock, with its vast views—stopping half-way up for a look at Gibraltar's famous Barbary apes. Legend has it that British dominance will end should the apes ever leave Gibraltar. When the primate population declined significantly during World War II, Winston Churchill himself showed concern, and the apes have been on special rations ever since.

# East to Almería

It takes a good hour to cover the 51 kilometres (32 mi) that separate Málaga and Nerja, axis of a wide-flung tourist area. Emerging from the industrial suburbs, you come to RINCÓN DE LA VICTORIA, where the people of Málaga forgather. Prehistoric man was here first. He occupied a cave on the Málaga side of the village known as Cueva del Tesoro (Treasure Cave). According to legend, five Moorish kings buried a treasure within... still to be found.

The neighbouring community of BENAJARAFE boasts beachfront restaurants, tennis courts, campsites and the inevitable *urbanizaciones*. Roses bloom in a park by the sea. High-rise TORRE DEL MAR is the gateway to the upland wine- and raisin-producing region of the Axarquía and its capital, **Vélez-Málaga**, a town of 40,000 just 4 kilometres (2½ mi) inland. Of Phoenician foundation, Vélez radiates out from a historic centre. A Moorish alcazaba dominates the heights, and there are two venerable churches: the Late Gothic Iglesia de San Juan Bautista and the Iglesia de Santa María, incorporating a section of the town's former mosque.

The coastal villages of MEZQUITILLA, LAGOS and EL MORCHE woo tourists with tennis courts, swimming pools and the obligatory *discoteca*. Here as elsewhere on the eastern coastline, self-catering accommodation has the edge over hotels and hostels. Once dedicated solely to fishing and agriculture, TORROX-COSTA now serves tourism, too. Resort complexes have sprung up alongside extensive Roman ruins (lighthouse, baths and fish-curing plant).

A detour a couple of kilometres inland takes you past TORROX proper into terraced hillsides planted with olives. A scattering of white farmsteads dots the hills. It can be pleasant to drive on to COMPETA, but the road is for confident drivers only, narrowing as it does to a mere 5 yards (4½ m), with no guard rails provided.

## Nerja and Environs

There's just one big international resort to the east of Málaga, and that's **Nerja** (population 30,000), where British, German and Scandinavian holidaymakers fraternize in the high season. Nightlife is lively, though less hedonistic than in Torremolinos, and the beaches are good, if less expansive on this rugged, rocky coast than

those to the west. With excellent opportunities for scuba diving and fishing, Nerja has a very real appeal for sportsmen, while the annual festival of music and dance gives the town a certain cultural tone.

Hotels and hostels cluster around the **Balcón de Europa**, a palm-fringed promenade built atop a cliff that juts out into the sea, dividing the sandy crescent of La Caletilla beach from that of La Calahonda. Nerja has several other strands, but they say the best of the lot is Burriana, over by the parador. Nerja's swinging restaurants and bars—many of them owned and operated by resi-

dent foreigners—constitute the resort's greatest attraction, together with a faintly traditional atmosphere. The occasional *burro* plods through the narrow central streets, transporting building materials or plastic vats of wine, and women in black stand eternally in the doorways.

An old centre of population, Nerja ("Rich Spring") acquired its name during the Moorish period. Its famous **cave** was discovered relatively recently, when a group of boys just happened on it one day in 1959, while they were out hunting bats. Signs lead motorists to the site, 4 kilometres (2 ½ mi) **51** east of town on the border of Maro village. You can also visit the grotto on an organized excursion. Tour operators all along the coast feature bus trips daily in season.

As if stalagmites and stalactites weren't enough, Nerja's cave has lights, music and action in the form of throngs of people filing through (smile for the cameraman as you descend...). On display in the first chamber are photographs of paintings discovered in the cave but not yet on view to visitors, some fragments of pottery and human bones of prehistoric vintage. (Occupied as early as 20,000 years ago, the cave was inhabited intermittently through the millenia until about 1800 B.C.) Don't miss the opportunity to attend a performance of the Nerja festival, held here below towards the middle of August.

In MARO itself, fields of tomatoes edge the sea, and the relatively isolated beach is the scene of nude bathing.

The corrugated hills of the Sierra Almijara form a textured backcloth to Nerja. The village of **Frigiliana** in these hills has become a residential suburb of the town, without altogether abandoning a traditional lifestyle. A rough, narrow road leads upwards: drive with caution, as you'll invariably encounter villagers on foot, donkey and moped heading home.

Under the Moors, Frigiliana counted among 22 prosperous villages of the Kingdom of Granada. Today the historic centre is regarded as one of the outstanding ensembles of Moorish village architecture on the Costa del Sol, with a 16th-century church and ruined Moorish castle to give it added cachet. Ascend the wide, cobbled stair-steps to the **mirador** (signs point the way) for a stunning overview of the village, its blinding-white, geometric houses surrounded by an apron of terraced fields, with Nerja and the sea in full view down below.

## The Far East

The pace of development is bound to pick up now that road improvements have been made on the eastern reaches of the N 340. From Nerja, the motorway weaves through the mountains, in sight of sheltered coves and a savage sea. For the time being, there's little traffic, few people, and hardly even a

*Climb up to Frigiliana's mirador for a vast view of the village.*

suggestion of construction to come. Swimming is from rocks or coved beaches, accessible by footpath or, more usually, by water only. The views of the ragged coastline are magnificent (surpassed only by the panorama from the old road that snakes up precipitously to the **Cerro Gordo** lookout). Some 20 kilometres (12 mi) from Nerja, LA HERRADURA's high-rise beachfront and the smart resort community of PUNTA DE LA MONA bring you back to civilization with a jolt.

Further along, the attractive beach development of **Almuñécar** is an adjunct to the old town, inviolate on its small hill. Port for Granada in Moorish times, Almuñécar continued to enjoy prestige after the Reconquest. Juan de Herrera, architect of Philip II's Escorial palace near Madrid, was commissioned to design the parish church, and its bell tower is the work of the great Diego de Siloé.

To get the feeling of the place, climb up through the narrow, dusty streets of the San Miguel quarter to the Moorish castle. With land inside the walls at a premium, the pragmatic people of Almuñécar long ago turned the courtyard of the fortification into a cemetery. Almuñécar has always been famous for its red pottery, and you can still see artisans at work here, turning out all manner of traditional pieces.

Just outside town, Almuñécar's **aqueduct** stands as a monument to the skills of the Roman engineers who constructed it during the reign of Emperor Antoninus Pius in the 2nd century A.D.

A scenic corniche road leads on for another 15 kilometres (9 mi) or so. Maritime pines bend in the wind as you loop through barren, undulating hills, devoid of all vegetation. At the end of the journey, white-walled **Salobreña** makes an impressive sight. Built on a rocky outcrop, the village is surrounded by fields of sugar cane. A restored Moorish fortress is Salobreña's crowning glory, while outside the walls, the modern resort hotels follow a mile and a half (3 km) sweep of sandy beachfront.

Industry takes precedence over tourism in the thriving port city of MOTRIL. Sugar cane

*Threshing grain the time-honoured way. For farmers of Andalusia, traditional methods work best.*

flourishes in the verdant *vega* (plain), all around and there are sugar refineries in the town, known to Spaniards as "Little Cuba". But pleasant beaches lie near at hand in TORRENUEVA, CALAHONDA and CASTELL DE FERRO. The **drive** from Calahonda to Castell de Ferro offers scenic attractions equal to any along the Costa del Sol. The road follows the tortuous shoreline in and out for 11 kilometres (7 mi) as earth, sky and sea come together.

Popular for years with Spanish holiday-makers, ADRA*, 37 kilometres (23 mi) on, is beginning to attract foreign tourists, too. In the meantime, the town remains an important fishing and fish-processing centre, with a distinguished history

---

* Although generally grouped with the Costa del Sol resorts, the holiday centres from Adra eastwards are also considered part of the up and coming Costa de Almería, which extends from Almerimar to Mojacar and beyond.

as a Phoenician colony and Roman port. Closer to Almería, ALMERIMAR, ROQUETAS DE MAR and AGUADULCE are expanding resort centres with good beaches and all the amenities.

## Almería

City of history and tradition, Almería has known some great moments. At its peak from the 8th to 11th centuries, the city's early importance gave rise to the saying, "When Almería was Almería, Granada was its farm". The Almería of today is a pleasant provincial town of 200,000, well worth visiting if your travels take you to the eastern limits of the coast—a distance of 222 kilometres from Málaga, or 138 miles.

There are but two major sights. The forbidding **cathedral** cum fortress stands just inland from the harbourfront *paseo*. Completed in 1524 as Barbary pirates continued their attacks, this bastion of the faith bolstered Almería's seaward defences.

Abd-er-Rahman III's **Alcazaba** looms large on the skyline. Although an earthquake in 1522 caused extensive damage, the crenellated ochre outer walls and a section of the turreted ramparts stand firm. From the citadel, wide-ranging vistas of the city and sea open out.

# Excursions Inland

There's so much to see so near to hand: Ronda, Jerez, Sevilla, Córdoba, Granada—all the great cities of Andalusia lie within easy reach of the Costa del Sol. If your time is limited, opt for one of the day trips organized in all the major resorts. Or strike out on your own at a more leisurely pace.

# Ronda

The opening of an improved road from San Pedro de Alcántara some years ago shortened the driving time from the coast to about an hour, ending the historical isolation of this mountain redoubt. Spectacular however you approach it, Ronda (population around 30,000) hangs high above a gorge that cleaves the city in two. The Moorish town *(Ciudad)* lies to the south, linked by an 18th-century bridge to Mercadillo, the district that evolved after the Reconquest.

The **gorge**, or Tajo, is a deep rent in the earth that plunges 490 feet (150 m) down to the surly Río Guadalevín, a tributary of the Guadiaro. During the Civil War Nationalist sympathizers in the town were hurled to their deaths in the abyss—executed without a shot being fired—an event recalled by Hemingway in his novel *For Whom the Bell Tolls*. You have a superb view of the Tajo and the patchwork of fields beyond from the **Puente Nuevo** (New Bridge), in continuous use since 1788—though it's just as impressive to look up at the gorge from below. (Follow the Camino de los Molinos into the void.)

Crossing the bridge into the **Ciudad**, you enter the old Moorish enclave, impervious to Christian assault until 1485. Bear to the right and continue along to **Plaza de Campillo**, another fine vantage point.

Out in the distance, you'll see vultures tracing slow circles above the grey, stony ridge of Ronda's mountain range, the Serranía de Ronda.

**Palacio de Mondragón**, to one side of the square, was the one-time residence of Ronda's Moorish kings—and its Christian conquerors. (Opening hours are capricious due to on-going restoration of the interior.) A Renaissance portal—a distinguished later addition—opens on to spacious courtyards where horseshoe arches, Arabic inscriptions and distinctive tile ornament indicate the real origins of this stately structure. Some of the rooms are out of bounds to visitors, but you can go into the garden

## Andalusia in Perspective

| | |
|---|---|
| *Geography:* | With an area of 34,700 square miles (90,000 sq km), Andalusia accounts for one-sixth of Spain's territory. It comprises the nation's eight southerly provinces and the southern Mediterranean and Atlantic coastlines. Principal mountain ranges are the Sierra Nevada and Sierra Morena. The most important river is the Guadalquivir. |
| *Population:* | 6½ million. |
| *Capital:* | Sevilla (population 600,000). |
| *Industries:* | Tourism, agriculture, mining. |
| *Religion:* | Roman Catholic. |
| *Language:* | Spanish. |
| *Climate:* | Mild in winter, hot and dry in summer. |

with its prolific pomegranate tree and up to the roof terrace where the king of the Moors was lord of all he surveyed.

A street or two away, Ronda's chief mosque survives as the church of **Santa María la Mayor**. The minaret was converted into a bell tower, and a Gothic nave was tacked on to the original structure, followed in time by a high altar in ornate 16th-century Plateresque style and some finely carved Baroque choir stalls. The church fronts on the Ciudad's main square, the expansive Plaza de la Duquesa de Parcent, shaded with cypress trees, shadowed with lamplight.

Heading back towards Puente Nuevo, stop off at the **Palacio del Marqués de Salvatierra**, a Renaissance mansion now used by this aristocratic family as a holiday house. Guided tours take place at half-hourly intervals, morning and afternoon, except when the family is in residence. As you approach, you can't help but notice the curious nudes above the entranceway. They are Inca Indians, a reminder that the house was built during the era of American discovery and conquest. In another allusion to those momentous times, a carved wooden doorway within **58** displays the portrait heads of

the great explorers, Columbus and Pizarro.

As you go through the richly appointed rooms, the guide will point out traditional pieces of furniture like the *vargueño*, or fall-front desk, with intricate marquetry detail, and the *brasero*, or brazier, that is Spain's age-old answer to the portable heater. Filled with hot coals and placed under a long-skirted table, the device warms the lower extremities of those who sit around it, brandy presumably taking care of the rest.

Beyond the house, the road curves down towards the Tajo, where two more bridges span the void: the Moorish **Puente Viejo** (Old Bridge) and **Puente San Miguel**, built on Roman foundations. Both offer striking views of the chasm. Down by the river stand the **Moorish Baths**, the vaulted roof intact.

The main sight in **Mercadillo** is Ronda's Neoclassical **Plaza de Toros**, one of the oldest bullrings in Spain. Inaugurated in 1785, it is regarded as the cradle of the bullfight and its cathedral (see p. 89). A small museum below the graceful, arcaded stands recalls the fabulous careers of the Romero

*Compact Ronda teeters precipitously above the Tajo.*

family of toreros and their 20th-century successors, the Ordoñéz clan.

South-west of town, a scenic route leads 25 kilometres (15 mi) through the fissured hills of the Serranía de Ronda to **Cueva de la Pileta** (follow the signs to BENAOJÁN). At the dawn of history, prehistoric man took shelter here (see p. 14). A guide equipped with a gas torch conducts visitors through eerie galleries that stretch for a mile under the earth. It's a good idea to bring along a torch of your own—to better illuminate the prehistoric art work that decorates the walls. Paintings of a bull's head and pregnant mare are among the oldest images. Realistically rendered in ochre and black, they date back 25,000 years to Paleolithic times.

*Your aperitif in the making: olives ripen while sherry matures in old oaken casks.*

# Jerez de la Frontera

The very name of the town means sherry—*jerez* (pronounced khay-*reth*). Wineries dominate Jerez de la Frontera, and vineyards surround it. Whether you visit Jerez with a group or on your own, you'll have plenty of opportunities to sample and purchase the famous wines produced here.

There are over 200 wineries, or *bodegas*, in this city of 150,000 people, among them the premises of the prestigious old firms: Garvey, Williams & Humbert, Pedro Domecq. As some of the names imply, it was a group of English merchants who launched Jerez as a world capital of wine. Three centuries on, their descendants continue to control the sherry trade.

Visitors to Jerez are welcome to see how the wine is made. All of the larger companies offer **free tours** of their *bodegas* weekly mornings. At Pedro Domecq they're proud to show

off casks with historic associations—both Lord Nelson and the Duke of Wellington drank the Domecq brand—while Gonzalez-Byass treats visitors to the sight of their wine-tippling mice. The hospitality of the *bodegas* is legendary: every tour ends with a tasting session.

Jerez is famous for horses, too. The **Andalusian Riding School** *(Escuela Andaluza de Arte Ecuestre)* was established in 1973 by the Domecq sherry family as a showcase for Andalusian equestrian skills. If you can't make it to Jerez for the annual spring horse show, try to see one of the dressage exhibitions here.

Among other major sights, Jerez's hill-top **Alcázar** stands out. Surrounded by gardens, the fortress rises above the central square, the Plaza de los Reyes Catolicos. Alfonso X stormed the citadel in 1264, and from that time forward Jerez remained in the Christian camp. "On the border" of the Kingdom of Granada, the town acquired the title by which it is still known: *de la Frontera*.

Below the Alcázar lies the **Collegiate Church** *(Colegiata)*, a towering dark stone construction of the 17th and 18th centuries. Housed within is the precious image of Christ of the Vineyards *(Cristo de la Viña)*.

# Sevilla

Capital of flamenco and the bullfight, Sevilla is the most Spanish of Spain's cities—the most spiritual, the most sensual, the most romantic. The white houses and tiled patios of the tourist posters are here, and the small squares with fountains and orange trees*.

Amerigo Vespucci and Ferdinand Magellan set out on their epic voyages from the port of Sevilla. Christopher Columbus lies buried here. Spain's great artists, Velázquez and Murillo, were born in the city. The story of Carmen unfolds in Sevilla, and so does that of Don Juan. Famous for the religious fervour of its Holy Week parades, Sevilla hosts Europe's liveliest spring fair a few weeks later, the *Feria de Abríl*.

Sevilla (population 600,000) was already a thriving riverside settlement when Julius Caesar came along in 45 B.C. Under the Romans, the settlement developed into a major town. Capital of the Visigothic kingdom for a time, and then of a Moorish *taifa*, Sevilla fell to Ferdinand III in 1248. A monopoly on trade with Amer-

---

* It's wise to divest yourself of all jewellery and valuables before you set out. Sevilla's pickpockets and thieves are notorious in Spain.

ica brought the city to its peak during the Golden Age. "Madrid is the capital of Spain", people said then, "but Sevilla is the capital of the world".

The Río Guadalquivir cuts a wide swath through the city centre, separating the monumental and commercial dis-

*Sevilla's Gothic cathedral: a treasure house of art and history.*

tricts on the left bank from the gypsy quarter of Triana on the right. If your time in Sevilla is limited, you'll want to concentrate on the highlights—the 63

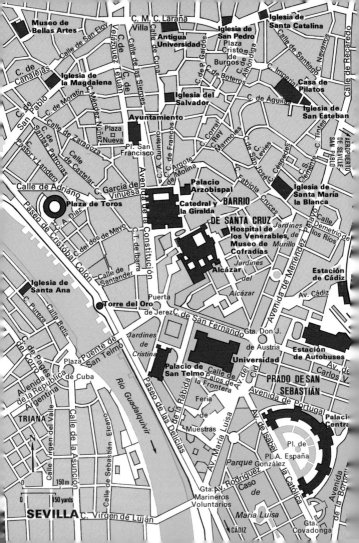

Cathedral, Giralda and Alcázar —all situated around Plaza del Triunfo on the east bank.

The largest Gothic church in the world, Sevilla **Cathedral** is a colossus of Christendom. Only St. Peter's in Rome and St. Paul's in London are bigger. In 1401, the people of Sevilla razed their great mosque to construct it. "Let us build a cathedral so immense that everyone on beholding it, will take us for madmen", church officials declared.

Massive without, richly decorated within, the Cathedral contains some precious works of art. There are over 30 chapels, including the central **Capilla Mayor** with its huge Flemish altarpiece, and the grandiose **Capilla Real** (Royal Chapel), last resting place of Ferdinand III, the "King Saint" who delivered Sevilla from the infidel. The silver-gilt key to the city presented to Ferdinand by the vanquished Moors may be seen in the treasury, along with a cross made of the first gold Columbus brought back to Spain from America. Appropriately enough, the Great Navigator himself is interred nearby. The ornate 19th-century sarcophagus near the south entrance contains his remains, transferred to Sevilla from Havana in 1898, when Cuba won independence from Spain.

On the north side of the cathedral lies the **Patio de los Naranjos** (Court of the Orange Trees), the ceremonial courtyard of the old mosque. Its minaret forms the base of the celebrated **Giralda** tower. Three distinct sections merge harmoniously: the sober 12th-century stonework at the bottom supporting a course of decorative brickwork, which is in turn capped by an ornate Renaissance bell chamber. Lofty symbol of Sevilla, the 322-foot (98-m) tower derives its name from the statue of *Faith* pivoting above it, for the figure serves as a weather vane *(giraldillo)*. Follow the ramp up to superb views of the town and its river.

Avenida de la Constitución leads north from the Cathedral to Sevilla's pedestrian shopping district, centred on the **Calle de las Sierpes**. East of the church extends the **Barrio de Santa Cruz**, the old Jewish quarter. This infinitely picturesque maze of white houses, narrow lanes and tiny squares invites leisurely exploration.

South of the cathedral in Plaza del Triunfo stands the former exchange building, Casa Lonja. Documents relating to the discovery and conquest of the Americas are on display within.

The **Alcázar** of Pedro the Cruel on the far side of the square is a major monument of the mid-14th century. The Mudejar architecture combines Moorish, Gothic and Renaissance elements. Executed by Moors to Moorish designs, the rambling palace and its several courtyards incorporates fragments of an earlier fortress.

A visit begins with a tour of the Admiral's Apartments *(Cuarto del Almirante)*, an addition constructed during the reign of the Catholic Monarchs, and the royal apartments, repeatedly remodelled down through the centuries. But you'll want to concentrate on the section surrounding the **Patio de las Doncellas** (Courtyard of the Maidens). The rooms here preserve outstanding decorative features from Pedro's time—ornamental tiles, carved stuccowork and characteristic coffered *artesonado* ceilings. The domed **Salón de Embajadores** (Hall of the Ambassadors) is equal to anything in the palace of the Alhambra, it is so richly embellished.

You'll also want to see the impressive **apartments of Charles V**, hung with Flemish tapestries and embellished with tile work. Superb in their own

right are the **gardens** of the Alcázar, scattered with pools and pavilions.

The Moorish **Torre de Oro** (Tower of Gold) stands down by the river. Tiles of gold once covered this chess-piece construction of 1220, all that remains of Sevilla's medieval fortifications. Pedro the Cruel used the tower as a prison. Now it houses a maritime museum.

To the south-east, the **Parque de María Luisa** borders the Guadalquivir. Horse-and-carriage rides through the bosky reaches of the park are a popular tourist activity. If that's not your style, try boating on the Plaza de España canal.

# Córdoba

They say that Córdoba is half Roman, half Moorish, and so it seems as you look out over the Guadalquivir for the first time, the tile roofs and whitewash of the Jewish quarter behind you, the great mosque to one side and the wide ribbon of the river ahead, its sluggish waters spanned by the stone bridge the Emperor Augustus built.

The Iberians founded a settlement here, but it was under the Romans that Córdoba first prospered. The town rose to even greater heights as capital of the caliphate of Córdoba. The second city of Islam, it was one of the great cultural centres of the medieval world (see p. 16).

Decline set in with the Reconquest, accomplished in 1236. The dismayed citizenry fled, and Ferdinand III took possession of a virtual ghost town. Even now, 750 years later, the population stands at less than 300,000—as opposed to half a million or more in its hey-day. Impoverished for centuries, the city developed only relatively recently, with the introduction of new industries and the expansion of mining activities.

The mosque, of course, is Córdoba's major sight. Many tourists have eyes for nothing else, but there are also several interesting museums in the vicinity, as well as an old synagogue and ruins of the Christian alcázar to explore.

Progressive restoration continues to reveal new facets of the edifice that is two houses of worship in one: cathedral and **Mosque** *(Mezquita)*. Abd-er-Rahman I erected the original shrine in the year 785. Thrice enlarged, the mosque achieved its present humbling proportions under Almansor (987).

No significant structural changes were made when the Christians first took over, but preservation of the architecture became a major issue in the 16th century after plans were announced to raise a cathedral within the mosque. Townspeople threatened workmen involved in the project with death, and Charles V himself was called on to officiate in the dispute. The emperor approved construction of the cathedral —to his eventual dismay. "You have destroyed something unique", he declared on seeing the church, "to build something commonplace." But the damage could not be undone, and Islam and Christianity have lived in peaceful co-existence ever since.

From the **belfry** that rises alongside you have a comprehensive view of the mosque's crenellated roofline, and the spires and buttresses of the cathedral perched uneasily atop it.

A high wall surrounds the sacred enclosure. Several gateways provide access, among them the monumental Mudejar **Puerta del Perdón**. You pass through the ceremonial forecourt with its fountains and orange trees *(Patio de los Naranjos)* to enter the mosque. Inside, mesmerizing rows of **columns** extend into the half-light in every direction. Antique shafts of porphyry, onyx, mar- 67

carved and coloured flat wooden ceiling, which was covered over with vaulting in the 18th century.

You literally have to go looking for the **cathedral**, the mosque is so large. But once you find it—at the very centre of the shrine's 6 acres (2 ha) —Islam fades completely from view. Jasper and marble gleam down from the high altar, and mahogany lends it lustre to choir stalls of 1750, a tour-de-force of Baroque carving. On the periphery of the cathedral, two Mudejar chapels of the 14th century echo the ornament of *mihrab* and *maksourah*: the **Capilla de Villaviciosa** (kept padlocked for the present), and the adjacent though not quite so resplendent Capilla Real. Other chapels line the perimeter of the mosque. A few of them are being dismantled, but no one will touch the Capilla de San Bartolomé, where Spain's great 16th-century poet, Luís de Góngora, lies buried.

A Christian king, Alfonso XI, built Córdoba's **Alcázar**, or what is left of it, south-west of the mosque on the river. It's amusing to clamber around the

ble, jasper, they seem to grow out of the paving stones like trees in an enchanted forest. The two-tiered arches overhead, striped red and white, form the most fanciful canopy of branches. And tendrils of stone twine round the splendorous 10th-century **mihrab** and the *maksourah* before it, the enclosure where the caliph attended to his prayers. In the central area of the mosque, restorers have exposed to view a section of the original

citadel and to go down below ground where ruins of baths *(baños árabes)* from the old Moorish palace have been discovered. But the real point of the exercise (be prepared to climb) is the **view** from the ramparts. The panorama takes in the old town and river, the islets of green in mid-stream (each with a ruined Moorish mill), and the blue belt of the Sierra de Córdoba, slung low on the horizon.

North of the mosque wind the narrow streets of the **Barrio de la Judería** (Jewish Quarter)*. Some of the best restaurants and *tapas* bars in Córdoba have premises in this evocative area, not just for tourists only. There's no hard and fast itinerary; you'll make your own discoveries as you wander about.

Sights to look for include the 14th-century synagogue *(sina-*

---

*Take the usual precautions against pickpockets and thieves, who make tourists visiting the old town a particular target.

goga) in the street called Judíos by the Moorish walls. It's a modest affair, just one small room with a balcony for women worshippers. Córdoba's Jews, unhappy under Visigothic rule, had helped the Moors to gain control of the city in 711, and they lived on in peace under the caliphate.

Perhaps the most illustrious resident of the neighbourhood was Moses Maimonides. A statue of the 12th-century doctor, philosopher and theologian stands a few steps from the synagogue in the square named in his honour, Plaza de Maimonides. The little Municipal Museum *(Museo Municipal de Arte Cordobesa y Taurino)* fronting on the square displays some examples of Córdoba craftsmanship (tooled leather, silver filigree) and mementoes of the bullfight.

North-east of the mosque, the splendid Renaissance Palácio Paéz shelters the **Museo Arqueológico Provincial**. A worthy array of artefacts spans the centuries from the Iberian era to Gothic times, but pride of place goes to objects salvaged from the ruins of the 10th-century palace of Medina Azahara, like the bronze figure of a stag that once adorned a fountain. Embossed all over with stylized "fur", this creature is from a bestiary, rather than the forest.

Ten kilometres (6 mi) northwest of town lies **Medina Azahara** or what remains of it. The one-time palace was commissioned in 936 by Abd-er-Rahman III for his favourite wife, Zahara, only to be laid waste by Berber soldiers in 1010. The reconstructed royal apartments give but an impression of the magnitude of this sumptuous complex of baths, schools, gardens and stately houses.

# Granada

There are two Granadas: the Moorish town, set high on the wooded bluff of La Sabica, and the Christian city founded at its foot. Of the monuments that once crowned the heights, only the Alhambra remains—a sprawling complex of fortifications, palaces and gardens from the 13th and 14th centuries that attests to the splendour of the kingdom of the Moors. On the plain below, the cathedral and Royal Chapel symbolize the glory of the Christian era that followed, ushered in by the Catholic Monarchs in 1492.

Organized tours of Granada begin on high with a full morning in the Alhambra, continuing down to the cathedral

and Royal Chapel in the afternoon. If you're visiting the city off your own bat, you'd be well advised to decide your priorities in advance—there's so much ground to cover. Some sights remain open through the lunch hour: the Alcazaba, the palace of the Alhambra and that of Charles V, as well as the palace and gardens of the Generalife. The Fine Arts and Hispano-Moorish museums, on the other hand, close for the day at 2 p.m., while the Royal Chapel opens mornings and after-

*Tourists bask in the reflected glory of the Alhambra.*

noons. One ticket, valid for two days, is good for admission to all the sights of the Alhambra, except for the museums.

The Nasrid dynasty rose to power in Granada as the fortunes of the Moors were waning (see p. 19). The first of the line, Mohammed ben Alhamar, established his capital here in 1232, after Ferdinand III forced him from Jaén. Two years later, Moors from a vanquished Sevilla swelled the population, already augmented by refugees from Córdoba. Rather than mourn for the homes they left behind, the industrious Moors set about making Granada the grandest city of all. And so, over the course of the next century, the precinct of the Alhambra took shape.

Ochre-red, rough-hewn, the palace of the **Alhambra** (Red Fort) rises at the very margin of the bluff where it stands. Massed above the valley of the Río Darro, its towers command superb views of the white, walled houses of the Albaicín quarter, and of the Sacromonte caves, where Granada's gypsies live. Look for the signs that point to the Alcázar, or Casa Real, as the palace is known in Spanish.

Entering through the former council chamber *(Mexuar)* and the small courtyard that adjoins it, you pass into the striking **Patio de los Arrayanes** (Court of the Myrtle Trees), where paired colonnades, clipped hedges, a reflecting pool and playing fountains make for a perfect Arabian Nights setting. The adjacent **Salón de Embajadores** (Hall of the Ambassadors), or royal audience chamber, is one of the most sumptuously ornamented rooms in the Alhambra. Skirted with tiling, the walls are overlaid with a fine tapestry of stuccowork that reaches 18 metres (60 ft) to the ceiling. Verses from the Koran and the name of the 14th-century monarch Yusuf I are woven into the design. Tall, horseshoe-shaped windows frame **views** of the Darro and Albaicín so magnificent that Charles V was moved to remark, "Ill-fated was the man who lost all this".

A gallery at the far end of the Court of the Myrtle Trees communicates with the enchanting **Patio de los Leones**. The name derives from the plashing fountain in the centre, upheld by twelve stone lions. A colonnade surrounds the fountain on four sides, its slender paired and single columns and projecting pavilions multiplying space to infinity. Splendid rooms radiate out on every side: the 73

**Sala de Abencerrajes** (notice the elaborate stalactite ceiling) recalls the aristocratic family of that name accused by Boabdil, last king of Granada, of disloyalty and collusion with the Christians. The king invited the Abencerrajes to a reception here which ended in the massacre of 36 family members.

Continuing to the right, ceiling paintings of Moorish and Christian kings at their leisure decorate the **Sala de los Reyes** (Hall of the Kings). The subject was taboo—Islam bans the images of men and animals from art—but the Nasrid kings were more influenced by Christian customs than the teachings of the prophet.

Right again, in the **Sala de las Dos Hermanas** (Hall of the Two Sisters), exquisite latticework shutters cover the windows, subduing the light. A wedding-cake cupola rises overhead, and the silvery overlay of stucco on the walls, incised with the greatest delicacy, is the icing on the cake. A pair of identical white marble slabs set in the floor on either side of the fountain are the "two sisters" of the title.

The lavishly decorated bedroom of the queen *(Mirador de Lindaraja)* juts out above a peaceful fountain court planted with cypress and orange trees.

On the opposite side of the court lie the **apartments of Charles V**, a suite of rooms renovated for the emperor, who shunned the arabesques of the Moors for the sober charms of an Italianate fireplace embellished with dolphins. This is where the novelist Washington Irving took up residence while composing his *Tales of the Alhambra* in 1829.

The modern Partal Gardens extend to the **Palace of Charles V** *(Palacio de Carlos V),* a structure that has been much maligned for its intrusive character—and for the fact that a section of the Alcázar was razed to make way for it. But considered on its own merits, the building must be regarded as a masterpiece of Renaissance architecture in Spain. Pedro Machuca, apt student of Michelangelo, designed this majestic circle in a square in 1526. The emperor, ever short of funds, financed it with a tax levied on the *moriscos* (see p. 20). Work on the building came to an abrupt halt when the converted Moors eventually revolted, and the palace remains unfinished to this day.

Two museums are housed within. The **Museum of Hispano-Moorish Art** *(Museo Nacional de Arte Hispanomusulmán)* displays such evocative artefacts as the throne of the Nasrids *(sillón del trono)*, an armchair of wood inlaid with silver and ivory, and the tombstone of the 15th-century king, Muley Hassan. His love for a Christian girl precipitated a civil war that set his son, Boabdil, on the throne and led to the fall of the kingdom. Highlight of the museum's exquisite collection of lustreware ceramics is that *chef d'œuvre* of the potter's art, the Alhambra Vase, which led a precarious existence for years in the Hall of the Two Sisters.

The Fine Arts Museum *(Museo de Bellas Artes)* chronicles the development of the school of Granada from the 16th to 19th centuries. Among all the works on display, there is one transcendent masterpiece, a still-life by Brother Juan Sánchez Cotán (1560–1627) entitled *Cardo y Zanahórias*. With a simplicity of means Sánchez Cotán conveys great depth of meaning, expressing all the harshness and beauty of the Andalusia region in this image of cardoons and carrots laid out on a stone window ledge.

Of the **Alcazaba**, the oldest part of the Alhambra, only the outer walls and towers survive. The main motive for a visit is the view from the Torre de la Vela of Albaicín and Sacromonte, silhouetted against the high peaks of the Sierra Nevada.

Accessible from the Alhambra enclosure by footpath and footbridge, the terraced gardens of the **Generalife** (Khay-nay-rah-*lee*-feh) ascend a neighbouring hill. The modest palace affords lovely views of the Alhambra, across the way. Oleander, rhododendron and roses thrive, fountains play and cascades tumble. If you approach via the north wall of the Alhambra, you'll see gardeners in gum boots opening and closing the sluices of the Moorish irrigation system that brings the life-giving waters of the Darro to these arid slopes.

Granada's white and gold cathedral is an imposing structure, but the exquisite, free-standing **Royal Chapel** (Capilla Real) to one side steals its thunder. The great masterpiece of Enrique de Egas, the Renaissance chapel serves as the mausoleum of the Catholic Monarchs. The façade, with its twisted columns and blind arcade, displays remarkable dignity and refinement, qualities that apply equally to the interior, its splendid wrought-iron **grilles** and marble **funerary monuments**. The effigies of Ferdinand and Isabella lie on the right-hand side of the chancel, with those of their daughter Joan the Mad and her husband Philip the Fair on the left. Their mortal remains repose in the crypt below, contained in simple caskets of lead.

Exhibited in the **sacristy** are Ferdinand's sword and Isabella's sceptre and crown, a circle of gold embellished with acanthus scrolls. On the walls hang superb 15th-century works of art from Isabella's personal collection, including Rogier van der Weyden's moving *Pietà* and his *Nativity*, an intimate, homely scene; an emblematic *Head of Christ* by Dierick Bouts; and Botticelli's *Christ in the Garden*, pious object of a queen's devotions.

A few steps from the chapel, the **Alcaicería**, the old silk market of the Moors, has been revived as a centre for handicrafts and souvenirs. An aura of times past lingers here and in the one-time Moorish district, the **Albaicín**, with ancient white houses, enclosed gardens and some stunning views of the Alhambra.

As advertised, the gypsies of Sacromonte still dance the flamenco in their caves, operating what is probably the world's best-known tourist trap. Don't let them lure you to one of their homespun spectaculars.

# What to Do

For most people, the beach is the end-all, be-all of a Costa del Sol holiday. But there are plenty of other ways to spend your time: shopping for Spanish handicrafts and leatherware, sampling *tapas* and wine, gambling at roulette, dancing in the streets—with a taste of bullfighting and flamenco for good measure.

## Sports

Golf, tennis, water sports—the Costa del Sol caters for them all. This is the place to improve your favourite sport or learn a new one.

### Water Sports

You can take your pick of activities if you base yourself in one of the major centres. Tourist beaches offer sports equipment for hire, as well as beach umbrellas and lounges. Larger beach restaurants *(merenderos)* have toilet facilities, and some provide changing rooms.

**Swimming**. With more than 100 miles (160 km) of beaches, the Costa del Sol offers plenty of scope for swimmers. Most of the sandy strands lie to the west of Málaga, while sand,

shingle and rock alternate to the east, where the mountains plunge steeply into the sea in places. You stand the best chance of having a patch of sand to yourself east of Nerja and west of Estepona. In the high season, the main beaches are mobbed, to say the least.

Topless bathing is very common now, and nudity is gaining ground, especially around Almería, at Maro in the Nerja area, at Marbella's Puerto Cabopino and around Tarifa. There's an authorized naturist beach at the Costa Natura colony, near Estepona.

Like other resorts in the Mediterranean, the Costa del Sol has had to deal with the problem of polluted waters and dirty beaches. Legislation has been introduced to discourage ships from dumping oil off the coast, and a sophisticated sewage treatment system has gone into operation, greatly improving the quality of the water.

**Boating**. You can set out to sea year-round on the Costa del Sol. From Almuñécar to Estepona, marinas provide harbourage for yachts and motor boats and, in some cases, make hire arrangements. Marbella alone boasts three ports: Puerto Banús, Puerto Deportivo and Puerto Cabopino. In addition, most tourist beaches and larger beach hotels have some kind of water craft for hire. You'll see plastic-hulled sailing dinghies all over. Easily manoeuvrable, these two-seaters are ideal for anyone learning to sail. You have to be fairly experienced to handle a catamaran. With a capacity of three or four, this sleek craft is built for speed. Rowing-boats are available most places, as are pedalos or water bicycles. Kayaks, fun for one, can be tricky to paddle.

**Water-skiing**. The main resorts all have water-ski schools, and most big hotels also offer instruction. Prices are generally high, but they do vary. You can save money if you shop around. Most schools give discounts for multiple runs paid in advance.

Try to go out early in the morning, when seas are calm and swimmers few. Swimming and skiing areas often overlap as the day goes by. So don't automatically expect a clear run if you are a power boat driver or a skier—even if you're in the reserved ski area.

**Windsurfing**. This is the coast's fastest-growing sport, with boards and tuition widely available. The season runs from March to November, though winds are generally at their strongest in June and September.

**Snorkelling and Scuba Diving.** Snorkelling can be an engrossing activity, particularly off the rocky, indented stretch of coast beyond Nerja. If you swim any distance from the shore, you are legally required to tow a marker buoy. Diving centres operate in several resorts. They provide boats and equipment, and, in some cases, tuition. They can also arrange for the necessary diving permits.

**Fishing.** Fishing from the rocks and casting into the surf doesn't always bring success: you'll improve your chances if you inquire locally about likely areas. Offshore waters teem with tunny (tuna), sea bass,

*It may take a while to make a catch, but there's always time on the Costa del Sol.*

swordfish and, around Marbella, shark. Deep-sea fishing boats can be hired at marinas, and many resort hotels make arrangements for fishing expeditions.

A popular fishing spot inland is the Chorro Dam (Pántano del Chorro). Freshwater fishermen must have a permit. Inquire at the tourist office for information on how to obtain one.

## Other Sports

**Golf**. When it comes to variety of courses and quality of instruction, few resort areas in the world can compare with the Costa del Sol. There are 13 major courses between Málaga and Estepona alone. Most private and hotel clubs welcome non-residents or non-members, though some may charge visitors a slightly higher fee. Clubs, caddies, trolleys and electric carts are generally available for hire.

For full details of golf courses and fees, consult the monthly magazine *Costa Golf*, an English-language publication, or the booklet "Golfing in Spain", issued by the National Tourist Organization.

**Tennis and Squash**. Some of the biggest names in tennis are linked to clubs, centres and "ranches" on the Costa del Sol, including Marbella-based Manolo Santana and Lew Hoad (Fuengirola). For details, consult monthly listings in *Lookout* magazine.

**Hunting**. The foothills of the sierra harbour wild rabbit and partridge, while deeper in the mountains lurk deer and wild goat, including the elusive *capra hispanica*. There are good hunting grounds in the area north of Marbella, especially in the Serranía de Ronda and, closer to the coast, the Sierra Blanca (see p. 46). The season for game runs roughly from September to December, while small animals may generally be hunted from October to February. A hunting permit is obligatory.

**Horse riding**. Andalusia is horse country, especially the inland area. But even on the coast, stables have some fine mounts for hire. You can canter along the open beach or ride up into the hills. Twelve-day tours of Andalusia are organized from Arcos de la Frontera. Inquire at the tourist office for details.

**Skiing**. Not everyone comes to the Costa del Sol to ski, but skiing there is at the Solynieve ("Sun and Snow") resort, 100 miles (160 km) north-east of Málaga in the Sierra Nevada. Situated up on Mt. Veleta, this is Europe's fifth highest and most southerly ski resort.

**Snooker (Pool).** The Fuengirola Snooker Club promotes the sport on the coast. There are plenty of places to play, for the club acts as an agent for the sale of snooker tables and equipment to clubs and bars all over.

## Shopping

Real estate may be the fastest-selling item on the Costa del Sol, but if you're not in the market for a holiday flat or *finca*, there are plenty of other things to look for here. Traditional Spanish handicrafts are high on any shopping list—ceramics,

basketry, wrought-iron work, rugs. Leather goods, while no longer the bargain they were, compare favourably in price with Italian- and French-made articles, and local factories turn out well-styled, high-quality leather clothing, available in the better boutiques.

Weekly open-air markets are a speciality of several coastal towns. Merchants, local and expatriate, purvey everything from recordings of the latest flamenco hits to clothing and garden produce, while all manner of bric-a-brac turns up at flea markets.

## Where to Shop

The city of Málaga offers lower prices and a greater selection of goods than resorts like Torremolinos or Fuengirola. You'll want to browse along the main shopping thoroughfares in the old town: Calle de Larios, Calle de Granada (a continuation of Larios) and Molina Lario. For sophisticated shopping, nothing can compare with Marbella or nearby Puerto Banús, where dozens of attractive, harbourfront boutiques offer a stunning selection of merchandise—for a price. Spain's leading department store chains operate branches in Málaga and larger towns.

## Buyer Beware

Wherever you shop, compare prices before you buy, as they can vary considerably. Don't forget that pickpockets and thieves plague Spain's shopping areas. Take the precautions outlined on page 110.

## Hours

Most establishments open from 9.30 or 10 a.m. to 1.30 or 2 p.m. and from 4.30 to 8 p.m. In summer, shops in the tourist resorts keep longer hours, until 8.30 or later. Department stores do not close for siesta. Some merchants in fashionable Puerto Banús do business through the lunch hour and evenings and Sundays, as well.

## Tax Rebates for Visitors

The Spanish government levies a value added tax (called "IVA") on most items. Tourists from abroad will be refunded the IVA they pay on purchases over a stipulated amount. To obtain the rebate, you have to fill out a form, provided by the shop. The shop keeps one copy; the three others must be presented at the customs on departure, together with the goods. The rebate will then be forwarded by the shop to your home address.

## Best Buys

**Basketry**. Alongside goods from Hong Kong and the Philippines, you'll see the authentic Andalusian article: sturdy shopping baskets, wine carriers, sombreros—even saddlebags of plaited straw.

**Brassware**. Look for hand-beaten bowls and pitchers in traditional forms.

**Ceramics**. The functional glazed terracotta pottery produced in Almuñécar and other towns can be purchased all

*Bargains in brassware abound on market day in Fuengirola.*

along the coast. There's also a wide selection of tiles, vases, bowls and jugs, with floral or geometric decorations.

**Cigars**. Imported Havanas round out the selection of Spanish cigars.

**Foodstuffs**. Carry away olives, olive oil, almonds, and *membrillo* or quince paste.

**Jewellery**. Silver rings, bracelets and necklaces in modern designs make good buys, as well as the artificial "Majorica" pearls of Spain. Look, too, for olivewood beads.

**Leather and suede**. Choose from a wide selection of handbags, belts and wallets, as well as some very attractive trousers, skirts, jackets and coats.

**Records and cassettes**. The selection of Spanish recordings ranges from *zarzuela* tunes and flamenco hits to classical works by Albeniz, Granados and De Falla.

**Rugs**. Durable and colourful Granada-style woollen rugs are cheaper in Granada than elsewhere. Some shops along the coast—particularly in the village of Mijas—make rugs and cushion covers to order.

**Souvenirs**. A growth industry, the fabrication of souvenirs knows no limits, no shame, from plastic castanets and imitation wine skins *(bota)* to bullfight posters printed with your name as matador.

**Wine and spirits**. Sweet Málaga wine, sherry and brandy—all available in a variety of decorative bottles—represent Spain's best bargain.

**Wooden articles**. Salad bowls, pepper mills and nutcrackers of olive wood make appealing gifts.

# Entertainment

The emphasis is on nightlife and lots of it. Many people come to the coast just for the discos and bars. Activities organized specifically for tourists enjoy perennial popularity, while traditional festivals and flamenco events attract a largely local following.

**Organized Outings.** Tour operators propose farmhouse barbecue parties (flamenco entertainment is optional) and lake swimming and boating excursions. *Burro* safaris, long a feature of Costa del Sol tourism, involve an hour's ride from a mountain village to a *paella* party out of doors. You can make bookings through your hotel or a local travel agent.

**Amusement Parks.** Visible from the N 340, Atlantis Aquapark in Torremolinos advertises "great family fun". The complex boasts a kamikaze water slide billed as Europe's highest, and a wave pool that generates six-foot (2-m) breakers. Waterfalls, whirlpools, beach areas and restaurant all contrive to pull in the crowds. Open daily from 10 a.m. to sundown.

Like its more illustrious Copenhagen namesake, Tívoli World (in Arroyo de la Miel, between Torremolinos and Fuengirola) offers nightclubs, restaurants and bars, in addition to all the usual rides and attractions. Open Easter to October, 6 p.m. to midnight.

**Bullfights.** The Costa del Sol has some good rings—notably at Málaga, Estepona and Marbella—but apart from Málaga, bullfights here are mostly second string. Promoters save their best talent for Sevilla, Córdoba and other prominent cities, where spectators are at their most demanding.

In the main centres, fights take place every Sunday during the March to October season. Smaller towns often stage fights on national holidays, during town fairs and religious festivals. You may be enthralled—or appalled—by the spectacle but whatever your reaction, you'll gain valuable insights into the country and the people (see p. 89).

For another perspective on the *fiesta brava*, watch a televised fight, complete with close-ups and instant replay.

**Discotheques and Night Spots.** Some discos open as early as 9 p.m., but most establishments don't gear up for business until 11 p.m. or midnight. They close late, too, around 4 or 5 in the morning. Roller discos, lively from late afternoon till 2 a.m. or so, have **85**

*In all the resort centres, flamenco shows are staged nightly for tourists.*

opened up in a couple of resorts.

Night-clubs *(salas de fiesta)* usually stage two shows an evening, one at about midnight or 1 a.m. and the other around 3 a.m. Depending on the club, the spectacle may feature flamenco performances, drag acts or girlie shows. Bars, piano bars, pubs and clubs pro-

vide musical entertainment on through the night. A young crowd gravitates to Nerja's night spots. Torremolinos has a reputation for low life, while Marbella's resident celebrities give that resort plenty of jet-set glamour.

**Flamenco.** In all the coastal resorts, flamenco shows are organized for tourists. These

Moorish and gypsy elements. There are two distinct types of flamenco: the *cante jondo* (deep song), an intense outpouring of emotion, and the animated *cante chico* (light song). And then there are the flamenco dances: the *fandango*, *tango*, *farruca* and *zambra* —performed to the staccato rhythm and counter-rhythm of hand-clapping *(palmadas)* and finger-snapping *(pitos)*, the drumming of heels *(zapateado)* and the compulsion of the castanets.

Andalusians maintain that flamenco can be understood, but not explained. There's nothing difficult about the music. You simply have to feel it.

**Casinos**. Two gambling establishments operate from 8 p.m. to 4 a.m.: the Casino Torrequebrada in Benalmádena-Costa (on the N 340) and the Casino Nueva Andalucía in Marbella's Hotel Nueva Andalucía, also on the coastal highway. In addition to American and French roulette, blackjack, *chemin de fer* and other games, the casinos have a bar, restaurant and night-club on the premises. Formal dress is required. Don't forget to bring your passport along for identification.

**Concerts**. From May to October, Tívoli World brings the stars of rock and pop to

*tablaos* can be entertaining, but performances have an element of show business that purists decry. To experience flamenco at its most authentic, you have to search out bars and small clubs for Spanish connoisseurs in Málaga or Sevilla.Touring dance companies often take part in summer festivals organized in many towns. Look in the local press for announcements of special events.

An ancient art form, flamenco combines Visigothic,

**87**

Torremolinos for concerts in the open air. The season's programme may include occasional performances of flamenco and *zarzuela* (Spanish light opera). Year-round town fairs and celebrations often include popular concerts, but there's little in the way of

classical music during the summer season. In winter, Málaga's symphony orchestra performs in the Conservatory of Music, and guest artists appear at Castillo El Bil-Bil in Benalmádena-Costa.

**Cinema**. In Spain, most films are dubbed into Spanish. A few cinemas screen films in the original language—notably the one at Puerto Banús, plus cinema clubs in Málaga and Marbella—but this is the exception, not the rule.

*Armed with steel-tipped darts,* banderillero *meets bull in the second act or* tercio.

# The Bullfight

Called a "ballet of death", Spain's national sport is a highly ritualized encounter between man and bull. In a typical contest, three matadors fight six bulls—menacing animals three to five years old, each weighing as much as half a ton.

The 2½-hour spectacle opens to the music of the *paso doble*: the matadors, dressed in their suits of lights, parade around the ring, followed by the members of their *cuadrilla* or team. Then, with the drop of a handkerchief, an official known as the *presidente* signals the start of the proceedings.

Each fight comprises three acts or *tercios*. The first act begins with the release of the bull into the ring. Members of the *cuadrilla*, followed by the matador himself, play the animal with wide magenta capes, testing its bravery as they display their own courage and agility. Immediately afterwards, the *picadores* ride into the ring on horses protected by padding. Armed with lances, they pierce the bull's neck muscles to weaken it and to lower its head for the kill.

The second act brings the *banderilleros* on to the scene. Running obliquely across the path of the bull, they plunge several pairs of beribboned steel-tipped darts *(banderillas)* into the shoulders of the bull, barely avoiding contact with the horns. This serves to further rouse the animal, while correcting any tendency to hook.

In the third and final "act of death" *(la suerte de la muerte)*, the matador steps alone into the ring. He taunts the bull with the small red cape or *muleta*, drawing it close to his body in a series of passes that provoke danger—or merely simulate it. Finally the moment of truth arrives. The matador advances for the kill, leaning over the horns to thrust the sword deep between the bull's shoulder blades, into the heart. After an exceptional fight, the matador may be awarded one or both of the bull's ears as a trophy, perhaps even the tail and a hoof.

But death in the afternoon isn't always swift or even sure. Very occasionally, a bull that displays extraordinary bravery is allowed to live.

Although Spain's medieval knights fought bulls on horseback, the *corrida* as we know it today did not evolve until the 18th century. Francisco Romero, a native of Ronda, was the first matador to use cape and *muleta*. His son, Juan, developed the role of the *cuadrilla*, and his grandson, Pedro, created the classical style of the Ronda school. To this day, some spectacular fights take place in Ronda, the birthplace of the bullfight.

# Calendar of Events

January
: *Cabalgata de Reyes* (Three Kings' Parade). Málaga. On the eve of Epiphany (Jan. 5), floats, bands and traditional costumed characters recall the visit of the Wise Men to the Christ Child.

March/April
: *Semana Santa* (Holy Week). General. Sombre processions of hooded penitents and religious images take place nightly the week before Easter. Most impressive in Sevilla and, to a lesser extent, Málaga.

April
: *Feria de Abríl* (April Fair). Sevilla. Horses and riders, bullfights and flamenco are the durable elements of Andalusia's most colourful fair.

April/May
: *Feria del Caballo* (Horse Fair). Jerez. Spain's horse lovers come out in force for events of all kinds, from races to carriage competitions.

May
: *Romería de San Isidro* (Pilgrimage of St. Isidore). Estepona, Nerja. Decorated carts and costumed riders parade in Estepona, while Nerja stages concerts, folk dancing and fireworks.

June
: *Corpus Christi*. General. Bullfights and fireworks enliven this national holiday, a big event in Málaga.

June/July
: *Festival Internacional de Música y Danza*. Granada. International artists perform out of doors in the Alhambra and the gardens of the Generalife.

July
: *Virgen del Carmen*. Coastal towns. Processions on the water pay tribute to the Virgin Carmen, patron saint of fishermen.

August
: *Feria de Málaga* (Malaga Fair). A funfair, circus, bullfights and flamenco events animate the first fortnight of the month.

: *Festival de España*. Nerja. The town's famous cave provides the venue for this subterranean celebration of the performing arts (music and dance).

September
: *Feria de Ronda* (Ronda Fair). The highlight of the fair is the *corrida goyesca*, a costumed bullfight held in Ronda's 18th-century ring.

: *Fiesta de la Vendímia* (Wine Harvest Festival). Jerez. A parade, bullfights, flamenco and horse events follow the blessing of the harvest.

# Eating Out

Food is typically Mediterranean yet has special cachet in this sunny region. Simple or sophisticated dishes are made with wonderful ingredients—from lush tomatoes and artichokes to excellent seafood, and chefs have a fine hand with herbs and spices. Frying in virgin olive oil is a speciality in Andalusia, producing airy-light results. Sherry from Jerez de la Frontera adds to the general delights—both as an aperitif and a sauce ingredient.

Catering managers too often seem to think that tourists crave tasteless "international" fare or faded reminders of home cooking. But good, honest Spanish food *is* available, if one delves into gastronomic matters a bit. Sometimes the most unassuming little places provide perfectly good and reasonably-priced dishes. *Tascas*, *tabernas* or bars neglected or given low ratings by official guide books may offer more delicious food to accompany drinks—for a reasonable price—than highly-rated establishments. Sherry aficionados can spend a whole evening making the rounds of humble bars to sip *fino* and nibble at endless *tapas* or cocktail titbits.

In the resorts excellent, unpretentious restaurants (called *merenderos* or *chiringuitos*) crop up along tiny roads leading to the beach—as well as on the beach itself. But grander

*Crab, shrimps, mussels, lobster— take your pick of the day's catch.*

places along the coast and to the north in Córdoba, Granada and Sevilla may be very good indeed, offering stunning views, garden settings and a romantic atmosphere as a bonus.

*Paradores*—state-run hotels, often in historical buildings—make a good bet for dining in an attractive setting. But, of course, they may be filled with other tourists. It's a good idea to make a reservation. Cabaret and flamenco dinners are a must at least once, though not for food. The fiery dancing will distract you from any boredom with what's on your plate.

The late eating hours in

Spain usually stun first-time visitors. Spaniards rarely sit down to lunch *(almuerzo)* before 2 p.m. or dinner *(cena)* before 10. However, most restaurants serve an hour or two earlier, and you do get quicker service if you arrive early.

Restaurants often offer a *plato del día*, a special dish of the day, at a reasonable price. Although service is included in the bill, it is customary to leave an additional tip.

### Breakfast

Spaniards make do with a summary cup of coffee, and perhaps a dry roll or some twisted fritters *(churros)*. Hotels may offer more: fruit juice, sausages, eggs and so on. Spanish expresso *(café solo)* is strong stuff, even with a touch of milk *(un cortado)*; for a milder drink ask for *café con leche*—coffee with milk, like French *café au lait*.

### Tapas

Every good bar offers a big selection of *tapas,* bite-sized morsels to accompany drinks, and the colourful array provides enough choice and substance for a whole meal—like a smorgasbord. The name comes from the practice, now almost vanished, of providing a free titbit with every drink. The food was served on a small plate traditionally used to cover the glass and came to be called *tapa*, which means lid.

Among dozens of items to choose from: sweet red peppers in olive oil with garlic, Russian salad, slices of sausage—both spicy *chorizo* and paprika-flavoured *salchichón*—or *jamón serrano* (cured ham), marinated mussels, clams, baby squid, *tortilla española* (Spanish omelette, with potato and onion filling, usually served cold in slices). One helping is called a *porción*. For a large serving of any given *tapa,* ask for a *ración*. If that's too much for you, order a *media-ración*.

### Soups

Speak of Spain to a food connoisseur and you're likely to hear all about *gazpacho*. An Andalusian speciality, it is now world-famous. There are dozens of ways to make it, but the version you are likely to find in southern Iberia is a creamy, chilled tomato and cucumber preparation with onion and garlic flavouring. On the side are freshly-diced green sweet pepper, tomato and cucumber, chopped hard-boiled egg, and fried croutons to add at will.

Originally from Málaga, *ajo blanco* (white garlic soup) is

a variation on the *gazpacho* theme. Ground almonds and garlic form the base of this hot-weather refresher, served ice-cold with a garnish of chopped almonds and grapes.

Be sure to try the mixed fish or shellfish soups, *sopa de pescado* or *sopa de mariscos*. Like French *bouillabaisse*, *sopa marinera* is based on the day's catch and seasoned to the chef's fancy—usually with lashings of tomato, onion, pimento or cayenne, garlic, white wine or brandy.

### Salads and Egg Dishes
Mixed salads turn up everywhere on the Costa del Sol. Tomato-cucumber and variations on the Niçoise-style—with olives and onions—are the most common types.

Egg dishes make popular starters. *Tortillas* (omelettes) may be filled with asparagus, tunny (tuna) and tomato purée. *Huevos a la flamenca* is a baked dish of eggs cooked on a sauce base of tomato, garlic and herbs—usually accompanied with diced ham or *chorizo*, fresh peas and sweet red pimento.

### Vegetable Dishes
Spaniards usually eat vegetables as a first course, rather than an accompanying dish. Don't pass up that great speciality of Andalusia, *alcachofas a la Montilla*—tender artichoke leaves cooked in a mixture of wine and beef broth thickened with flour and seasoned with mint, garlic and saffron. *Judías verdes con salsa de tomate*, green beans in tomato sauce, redolent of garlic, can be very good. Also popular and available: peas *(guisantes)*, lentils *(lentejas)*, spinach *(espinacas)*, broad beans *(habas)*.

### Paella
The Spanish dish *par excellence* must be discussed on its own, since it involves a variety of ingredients, the main background provided by saffron-flavoured rice, olive oil, seafood and chicken. But every chef has his personal variation of this colourful dish that originated around Valencia on Spain's eastern coast. The secret is fresh produce—whether or not it includes *langosta* (spiny lobster), *langostinos* (a kind of large shrimp), *cigalas* (Dublin Bay prawns or sea crayfish), *gambas* (prawns), mussels, chicken, peas, bell peppers or artichoke hearts. The name *paella* comes from the flat, round metal pan it is cooked in, and aficionados say that cookout-style, over an open fire, is the only way to prepare this hearty dish.

## Seafood

Fish and shellfish are a natural choice on the Costa del Sol. For starters, Spaniards like eel *(anguila)*, often served as a mousse or pâté. Squeamish eaters cringe and connoisseurs rave about squid in its ink *(calamares en su tinta)*, a spicy dish well worth trying. *Gambas* and *cigalas* are tantalizing grilled fresh from the sea *(a la plancha)*.

When available, the *langosta* is excellent hot with butter or cold with mayonnaise, but it never comes cheap. The quick fish-fry is renowned. Try *boquerones* (fresh anchovies), *chopitos* (baby squid) or *calamares*. A mixed fish fry, *fritura malagueña*, includes all of the above and more.

*Merluza,* or hake, may be served fried, boiled, or mushroom-stuffed, perhaps with tomatoes and potatoes. *Besugo* (sea bream) is a high-quality fish, brushed with olive oil and grilled. Don't run if you see *rape* on the menu; pronounced *rah*-pay, it's monkfish or angler-fish, with firm-fleshed tail meat that can taste like lobster.

## Chicken and Meat

Chicken is usually tasty, especially braised in white wine or sherry with almonds. The staple *arroz con pollo* (chicken with rice) is good if your *pollo* is farm-fresh and treated with respect.

Typical Andalusian preparations include *riñones al Jerez*, kidneys sautéed with sherry, and *rabo de toro* (oxtail) braised and served in a rich sauce containing carrots and spices. *Ternera a la Sevillana*, veal in sherry sauce with green olives, is a speciality of Sevilla. Rabbit *(conejo)* or hare *(liebre)* turn up in various casseroles in the autumn.

Steak and various cuts of beef are available—although not quite on a par with what's served in the Argentine or Texas. An original version is *bistec a la mantequilla de anchoas* (beefsteak with anchovy-butter sauce).

## Cheese, Desserts

Spaniards sometimes eat cheese *(queso)* after the main course, notably the tangy *queso de manchego*—fresh, smoked or in oil—and the milder *queso de Burgos*, widely available on the coast. You may also come across *queso de cabrales*, a combination cheese made from goat, cow and sheep milk in the north-western province of Asturias. After ageing, it is blue-veined and has a sharp taste, rather like Roquefort. *Idiázabal* is goat cheese smoked and cured.

The cornucopia of fruits in season includes grapes *(uvas)*, figs *(higos)*, melon *(melón)*, oranges *(naranjas)*, custard apples *(chirimoyas)*, strawberries *(fresas)* and cherries *(cerezas)*.

Besides myriad ices and ice creams, southern Spain offers pastries and cream desserts in abundance. One appealing preparation is *brazo de gitano*, a rolled sponge cake with a rum-flavoured, cream filling. *Flan*, or egg custard with caramel sauce, invariably appears on menus all over Spain. Eggs may also be cooked with sugar in a thickened custard called *natillas*.

## Wine and Spirits

Spain produces many honourable-to-very-good wines. *Sangría* needs little introduction, as it is already world-famous. The iced combination of red wine, brandy, lemon, orange and apple slices makes a great refresher for beach or terrace throughout the day. It can pack a punch, so you might want to add some soda water.

An aristocrat among wines, sherry *(jerez)* is grown in chalky vineyards around Jerez de la Frontera. It is aged according to centuries-old tradition in long stacked rows of casks or butts, by blending young wine

with a touch of older ones—a method known as *solera*.

*Fino*, the driest of sherries, is a light, golden aperitif which should be served chilled. A type of fino, *manzanilla* has a slightly richer quality; it's especially good in Sanlúcar de Barrameda where it is made.

*Amontillado*, usually me- **97**

dium dry, is a deeper gold colour and heavier than a true fino. *Amoroso* is medium sweet, of an amber colour. And *oloroso* is usually more full-bodied. Cream sherries are deeper coloured and sweet.

Andalusia produces several other semi-sweet to sweet wines, notably the sweet wine of Málaga, called *Málaga dulce* (rather like port), and that from Montilla-Moriles, made near Córdoba.

Wine is produced all over Spain, but the most famous is Rioja from the Ebro valley to the north. The white wines of Rioja, dry or sweet, are considered quite drinkable. But Rioja red is the glory of Spain; the aged Gran Reservas (5 years or more) are comparable to some of France's noblest red wines, though experts find that Riojas have a character all their own and do not necessarily resemble Bordeaux or Burgundy.

Look also for red wines that carry the Marqués de Riscal label. At all price levels of varying quality, they are always good. Siglo, CUNE, Berberana and Campo Viejo are reliable labels for table wines in white, red and excellent rosé.

Navarre, north of the Ebro valley, also produces some interesting red wines (look for Campanas, Murchante, Seño-

rio de Sarría). From La Mancha between Madrid and Andalusia come Valdepeñas wines, which are light, crisp, pleasing —a staple for *sangría*. Reds and whites from Catalonia figure, too, on Costa del Sol wine lists. Labels to look for include Torres and Rene Barbier. For casual dining and with economy in mind, ask if the restaurant has its own table wine—*vino de la casa*— which can be quite decent and inexpensive.

Spain also makes a mass-produced sparkling wine of the champagne type, referred to as *Cava,* which may be on the sweet side. Among the best are Gran Cordorniu or Cordorniu Non Plus Ultra. Sparkling *espumosos* can be equally refreshing on a warm day.

Spanish brandy or cognac tends to be heavy, but it is usually drinkable and reasonably priced. The relatively more expensive brands prove quite smooth. The many liqueurs available are often foreign brands made in Spain under licence. People on holiday like to try them because they are much less expensive than on their home territory. Many have a highly herbal flavour. The various anis-flavoured drinks *(anís)* resemble Greek *ouzo* or French *pastis*.

## To Help You Order...

Could we have a table?  ¿Nos puede dar una mesa?
Do you have a set menu?  ¿Tiene un menú del día?

I'd like a/an/some...  Quisiera...

| | | | |
|---|---|---|---|
| beer | una cerveza | milk | leche |
| bread | pan | mineral water | agua mineral |
| coffee | un café | napkin | una servilleta |
| cutlery | los cubiertos | potatoes | patatas |
| dessert | un postre | rice | arroz |
| fish | pescado | salad | una ensalada |
| fruit | fruta | sandwich | un bocadillo |
| glass | un vaso | sugar | azúcar |
| ice-cream | un helado | tea | un té |
| meat | carne | (iced) water | agua (fresca) |
| menu | la carta | wine | vino |

## ...and Read the Menu

| | | | |
|---|---|---|---|
| aceitunas | olives | judías | beans |
| albóndigas | meat balls | langosta | spiny lobster |
| almejas | baby clams | langostinos | large prawns |
| atún | tunny (tuna) | lenguado | sole |
| bacalao | cod | mariscos | shellfish |
| besugo | sea bream | mejillones | mussels |
| boquerones | fresh anchovies | melocotón | peach |
| calamares | squid | merluza | hake |
| callos | tripe | ostras | oysters |
| cangrejo | crab | pastel | cake |
| cerdo | pork | pimiento | sweet red pepper |
| champiñones | mushrooms | | |
| chorizo | a spicy pork sausage | pollo | chicken |
| | | pulpitos | baby octopus |
| chuletas | chops | queso | cheese |
| cigalas | Dublin Bay prawns | salchichón | salami |
| | | salmonete | red mullet |
| cordero | lamb | salsa | sauce |
| entremeses | hors-d'œuvres | ternera | veal |
| gambas | prawns | tortilla | omelette |
| huevos | eggs | trucha | trout |
| jamón | ham | uvas | grapes |

# BLUEPRINT for a Perfect Trip

## How to Get There

Before you plan your trip to the Costa del Sol, consult a reliable travel agent for up-to-the-minute information on fares and special tickets.

## BY AIR

### Scheduled flights

Direct flights link certain European cities to Málaga's Aeropuerto Internacional, air gateway to the Costa del Sol. Connecting service from cities throughout Europe and North Africa operates via Madrid's Barajas airport, which is the main point of entry to Spain for transatlantic and intercontinental travellers.

### Charter flights and package tours

**From the U.K. and Ireland:** Choose from a wide selection of package tours and flight-only arrangements. Many tour operators recommend cancellation insurance, a modestly priced safeguard: you lose no money if illness or accident forces you to cancel your holiday.

**From North America:** The Costa del Sol is included in some Iberian or European packages that allow you to visit several Spanish cities during a specified period of time.

**From Australia and New Zealand:** There are no package tours to the Costa del Sol, though the region is featured on some general tours of Spain.

## BY ROAD

The main access roads from France are at the western and eastern ends of the Pyrenees. On the western route, travel is by motorway (expressway) from Biarritz (France) to Burgos. From there, you take the N-1 to Madrid and the N-IV to Bailén, continuing either on the N-323 south via Granada to the coast or on the N-IV south-west to Córdoba (then south again to Málaga) or Sevilla (southwards to Cádiz).

From Perpignan in south-eastern France, you can follow the motorway south via Barcelona to Alicante or take the more scenic coastal road, continuing on the E-26 via Murcia to Granada or the E-26 to Puerto Lumbreras and N-340 to Almería.

A long-distance car-ferry service operates from Plymouth to Santander in northern Spain (a 24-hour trip); from Santander, follow the N-623 to Burgos and proceed as described above.

## BY RAIL

There is a direct connection Paris–Algeciras. For Málaga, take the direct Paris–Madrid train and change to the *Talgo* for the Costa del

Sol, a journey of 26 hours. Seat and sleeper reservations are compulsory on most Spanish trains.

The Spanish Tourist Office can give you details on discounted fares within Spain. The *Inter-Rail Card,* for example, permits 30 days of unlimited rail travel in participating European countries to people under 26. And the *Rail Europ Senior Card,* available to senior citizens, entitles the holder to discounts on European and internal Spanish rail journeys. Anyone living outside Europe and North Africa can purchase a *Eurailpass* for unlimited rail travel in 16 countries including Spain (sign up before you leave home).

# When to Go

Plenty of hot sunshine and cloudless skies—that's the rule, not the exception on the Costa del Sol. There are, nevertheless, seasonal variations worth noting as you choose your holiday time.

From June to September, hot days with low humidity are only occasionally broken by cooler evenings. In April, May and October daytime temperatures remain quite warm. From November through March—darkest winter in much of Europe—shirtsleeve sunshine is still to be found on the Costa del Sol. But the normally balmy days may be interrupted by chill winds from the mountains and that rare local phenomenon—rain.

Note that summer temperatures are much higher inland than along the coast, while the coastal resorts tend to be warmer in winter thanks to the protection offered by the mountain ranges.

Following are average monthly temperatures for Málaga.

|  |  | J | F | M | A | M | J | J | A | S | O | N | D |
|---|---|---|---|---|---|---|---|---|---|---|---|---|---|
| °C max. |  | 16 | 17 | 18 | 20 | 23 | 25 | 28 | 29 | 26 | 23 | 19 | 17 |
| min. |  | 10 | 11 | 12 | 13 | 15 | 18 | 20 | 21 | 19 | 17 | 14 | 11 |
| °F max. |  | 60 | 62 | 65 | 68 | 73 | 78 | 83 | 83 | 79 | 73 | 66 | 62 |
| min. |  | 50 | 51 | 54 | 56 | 60 | 64 | 68 | 69 | 67 | 62 | 57 | 53 |
| sea tempera- | °C | 15 | 14 | 15 | 16 | 17 | 21 | 21 | 23 | 21 | 18 | 17 | 14 |
| tures | °F | 59 | 57 | 59 | 60 | 62 | 69 | 69 | 73 | 69 | 65 | 62 | 57 |

# Planning Your Budget

To give you an idea of what to expect, here's a list of some average prices in Spanish pesetas (ptas.). They can only be *approximate*, however, as prices vary from place to place, and inflation in Spain, as elsewhere, creeps relentlessly up. Prices quoted may be subject to a VAT/sales tax (IVA) of either 6 or 12%.

**Baby-sitters.** 400–750 ptas. per hour.

**Camping.** *De luxe:* 450–550 ptas. per person per day, 2,000–3,000 ptas. for a tent or caravan (trailer) or mobilehome. *3rd category:* 300–400 ptas. per person, 650–800 ptas. for a tent or caravan. Reductions for children.

**Car hire.** *Seat Ibiza* 2,100 ptas. per day, 21 ptas. per km., 25,000 ptas. per week with unlimited mileage. *Ford Escort 1.1 L* 2,600 ptas. per day, 25 ptas. per km., 40,000 ptas. per week with unlimited mileage. *Ford Sierra 2.0* (automatic) 4,700 ptas. per day, 47 ptas. per km., 54,000 ptas. per week with unlimited mileage. Add 12% VAT.

**Cigarettes.** Spanish 60–115 ptas. per packet of 20, imported from 175 ptas.

**Entertainment.** Cinema from 300 ptas., flamenco nightclub (entry and first drink) from 2,000 ptas., discotheque from 1,000 ptas.

**Hairdressers.** *Woman's* haircut, shampoo and set or blow-dry 1,200–4,000 ptas. *Man's* haircut 800–2,000 ptas.

**Hotels** (double room with bath). \*\*\*\*\* from 10,000 ptas., \*\*\*\* from 9,000 ptas., \*\*\* from 6,000 ptas., \*\* from 4,000 ptas., \* from 2,800 ptas. Add VAT.

**Meals and drinks.** Continental breakfast 350–500 ptas., *plato del día* from 500 ptas., lunch/dinner in good establishment from 1,500 ptas., beer (small bottle or glass) 60–100 ptas., coffee 60–100 ptas., Spanish brandy 80–200 ptas., soft drinks from 100 ptas.

**Shopping bag.** Loaf of bread 35–120 ptas., 250 grams of butter 325 ptas., dozen eggs from 140 ptas., 1 kilo of steak 1,500 ptas., 250 grams of coffee 300 ptas., 100 grams of instant coffee 360 ptas., 1 litre of fruit juice 180 ptas., bottle of wine from 100 ptas.

**Sports.** *Golf* (per day) green fee from 3,000 ptas., caddie fee 1,000 ptas. *Tennis* court fee 500 ptas. per hour, instruction from 1,000 ptas. per hour. *Windsurfing* from 1,200 ptas. per hour. *Horseback riding* 1,000 ptas. per hour.

**Taxi.** Meters start at 70 ptas. Long distances negotiable.

# An A–Z Summary of Practical Information and Facts

> A star (*) following an entry indicates that relevant prices are to be found on page 103.
>
> Listed after some basic entries is the appropriate Spanish translation, usually in the singular, plus a number of phrases that should help you when seeking assistance.

**A**

**AIRPORT** *(aeropuerto)*. The Costa del Sol is served by Málaga's Aeropuerto Internacional, some 8 kilometres from the centre of Málaga, 7 kilometres from Torremolinos.

Porters are available to carry your bags to the taxi rank or bus-stop. They wear a badge which states their rate.

The airport has a tourist information office, a post office and a currency-exchange counter. There are bus services every 30 minutes to Málaga, Torremolinos and Benalmádena-Costa, as well as a half-hourly train connection to the coastal resorts between Málaga and Fuengirola.

Some visitors use Gibraltar airport, linked by scheduled flights to Great Britain.

| | |
|---|---|
| Porter! | ¡Mozo! |
| Taxi! | ¡Taxi! |
| Where's the bus for...? | ¿De dónde sale el autobús para...? |

**B**

**BABY-SITTERS\***. This service can usually be arranged with your hotel. Rates may vary considerably but are generally lower in the quieter resort areas. In most places they go up after midnight.

| | |
|---|---|
| Can you get me a baby-sitter for tonight? | ¿Puede conseguirme una canguro para cuidar los niños esta noche? |

**BICYCLE and MOPED HIRE** *(bicicletas/velomotores de alquiler)*. Bicycles can be hired in Torremolinos and Fuengirola. Elsewhere, they are hard to come by. You can hire one on a daily or weekly basis.

Several garages that rent bicycles also rent mopeds, and of course the rates are considerably higher. Insurance is obligatory and costs extra. Be prepared to lay out a deposit. Finally, remember that the minimum age for riding a motorcycle or moped under 75 cc. is 16; for vehicles over 75 cc., 18 (plus driving licence); and that the wearing of crash helmets is compulsory, whatever the capacity of the engine.

| | |
|---|---|
| I'd like to hire a bicycle. | **Quisiera alquilar una bicicleta.** |
| What's the charge per day/week? | **¿Cuánto cobran por día/semana?** |

**CAMPING\*** *(camping).* There are official campsites up and down the Costa del Sol, including Torremolinos, Marbella and Estepona. Ask permission before camping on private land.

Facilities vary, but most sites have electricity and running water. Many have shops and children's playgrounds, and some even launderettes and restaurants. Rates depend to a large extent on the facilities available.

For a complete list of camping sites, consult any Spanish National Tourist Office (see page 123).

| | |
|---|---|
| May we camp here? | **¿Podemos acampar aquí?** |

**CAR HIRE\*** *(coches de alquiler).* See also DRIVING. There are car hire firms in most tourist resorts and main towns. The most common type of car available for hire is the *Seat,* which has several models. The rates given on page 103 are sample prices of major operators. Local firms often charge considerably less. When hiring a car, ask for any available seasonal deals.

A deposit, as well as an advance payment of the estimated rental charge, is generally required, although holders of major credit cards are normally exempt from this. A tax is added to the total bill. Third-party insurance is automatically included.

Normally you must be over 21 and hold an International Driving Permit or a legalized and certified translation of your home licence. In practice, British, American and European licences are accepted in almost all situations.

| | |
|---|---|
| I'd like to hire a car (tomorrow). | **Quisiera alquilar un coche (para mañana).** |
| for one day/a week | **por un día/una semana** |
| Please include full insurance. | **Haga el favor de incluir el seguro a todo riesgo.** |

**C** **CIGARETTES, CIGARS, TOBACCO*** *(cigarrillos, puros, tabaco)*. Spanish cigarettes can be made of strong, black tobacco *(negro)* or light tobacco *(rubio)*. Tabacalera S.A. is the government tobacco monopoly, which supplies its official shops *(tabacos)*. Cigarette shops often sell postage stamps, too.

Locally made cigars are passable and cheap; among the better cigars, those from the Canary Islands are excellent.

Cuban cigars are available nearly everywhere and are a real bargain.

Most visitors to Spain consider local pipe tobacco a little rough.

| | |
|---|---|
| A packet of.../A box of matches, please. | **Un paquete de.../Una caja de cerillas, por favor.** |
| filter-tipped | **con filtro** |
| without filter | **sin filtro** |

**CLOTHING.** From June to September the days are always hot, but evenings sometimes turn cool, so take a jacket or cardigan. During the rest of the year evenings are generally cool, and a cold wind can upset the benign climate.

Sober clothing should, of course, be worn when visiting churches, but women are no longer expected to cover their heads.

**COMMUNICATIONS**

**Post offices** are for mail and telegrams; normally you cannot make telephone calls from them.

**Hours** vary slightly from town to town, but routine postal business is generally transacted:

from 9 a.m. to 1 or 1.30 p.m. and 4 to 6 or 7 p.m., Monday to Friday. Mornings only on Saturday.

Postage stamps *(sello)* are also on sale at tobacconists' *(tabacos)* and often at hotel desks.

If you see a mailbox marked *extranjero*, it is for foreign-destination mail.

**Poste restante (general delivery):** If you don't know ahead of time where you'll be staying, you can have your mail addressed poste restante *(Lista de Correos)* to whichever town is most convenient:

Mr. John Smith
Lista de Correos
Torremolinos
Spain

Take your passport to the post office as identification.

**Telegrams:** As mentioned above, post offices handle telegrams, but you can of course phone a telegram (tel. 22 20 00 in Málaga) or ask your hotel receptionist to do it for you. In Málaga, go to the main office in:

Paseo del Parque, open 24 hours a day.

Night letters or night-rate telegrams *(telegrama de noche)* are delivered the following morning and cost much less than straight-rate messages.

**Telephone** *(teléfono):* In addition to the telephone office in Málaga there are call boxes (phone booths) everywhere from which you can make local and international calls. Area codes for different countries are displayed in booths. You'll need a supply of small change. For international direct dialling, pick up the receiver, wait for the dial tone, then dial 07, wait for a second sound and dial the country code, city code and subscriber's number.

To reverse the charges, ask for *cobro revertido.*

For a personal (person-to-person), call, specify *llamada personal.*

| Spelling Code | | | | | | | |
|---|---|---|---|---|---|---|---|
| **A** | Antonio | **G** | Gerona | **M** | Madrid | **S** | Sábado |
| **B** | Barcelona | **H** | Historia | **N** | Navarra | **T** | Tarragona |
| **C** | Carmen | **I** | Inés | **Ñ** | Ñoño | **U** | Ulises |
| **CH** | Chocolate | **J** | José | **O** | Oviedo | **V** | Valencia |
| **D** | Dolores | **K** | Kilo | **P** | París | **W** | Washington |
| **E** | Enrique | **L** | Lorenzo | **Q** | Querido | **X** | Xiquena |
| **F** | Francia | **LL** | Llobregat | **R** | Ramón | **Y** | Yegua |
| | | | | | | **Z** | Zaragoza |

| | |
|---|---|
| Where is the (nearest) post office? | **¿Dónde está la oficina de correos (más cercana)?** |
| Have you received any mail for…? | **¿Ha recibido correo para…?** |
| A stamp for this letter/ postcard, please. | **Por favor, un sello para esta carta/tarjeta.** |

| express (general delivery) | **urgente** |
| airmail | **vía aérea** |
| registered | **certificado** |
| I want to send a telegram to… | **Quisiera mandar un telegrama a…** |
| Can you get me this number in…? | **¿Puede comunicarme con este número en…?** |

**COMPLAINTS.** By law, all hotels and restaurants must have official complaint forms *(hoja de reclamaciones)* and produce them on demand. The original of this triplicate document should be sent to the regional office of the Ministry of Tourism, one copy remains with the establishment complained against and you keep the third sheet. Merely asking for a complaint form is usually enough to resolve most matters, since tourism authorities take a serious view of complaints and your host wants to keep both his reputation and his licence.

In the rare event of major obstruction, when it is not possible to call in the police, write directly to the Consejería de Turismo de la Junta de Andalucía:

Apartado 152, Benalmádena-Costa.

New legislation has been introduced that greatly strengthens the consumer's hand. Public information offices are being set up, controls carried out, and fallacious information made punishable by law. For a tourist's needs, however, the tourist office, or in really serious cases, the police would normally be able to handle or, at least, to advise where to go.

**CONSULATES** *(consulado)*

| **Canada:** | Plaza de Malagueta, 3, Málaga; tel. 22 33 46. |
| **Great Britain\*:** | Calle Duquesa de Parcent, 3, Málaga; tel. 21 75 71. |
| **U.S.A.:** | Consular Agency: Edificio El Ancla, Hab. 502, Calle Ramón y Cajal, s/n, Fuengirola; tel. 47 48 91. |

Almost all Western European countries have consulates in Málaga. All embassies are located in Madrid.

* Also for citizens of Commonwealth countries.

If you run into trouble with authorities or the police, consult your consulate for advice.

| | |
|---|---|
| Where is the American/British/Canadian consulate? | **¿Dónde está el consulado americano/británico/canadiense?** |
| It's very urgent. | **Es muy urgente.** |

**CONVERTER CHARTS.** For fluid measures, see page 111. Spain uses the metric system.

**Temperature**

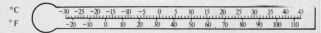

**Length**

**Weight**

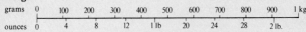

**COURTESIES.** See also MEETING PEOPLE. Politeness and simple courtesies still matter in Spain. A handshake on greeting and leaving is normal. Always begin any conversation, whether with a friend, shop girl, taxi-driver, policeman or telephone operator with a *buenos días* (good morning) or *buenas tardes* (good afternoon). Always say *adiós* (goodbye) or, at night, *buenas noches* when leaving. *Por favor* (please) should begin all requests.

Finally, don't try to rush Spaniards. They have no appreciation for haste, and consider it bad form when anyone pushes them on. Take your time. In Spain, there's plenty of it.

| | |
|---|---|
| How do you do? | **Encantado de conocerle (Encantada** when a woman is speaking**).** |
| How are you? | **¿Cómo está usted?** |
| Very well, thank you. | **Muy bien, gracias.** |

**C** **CRIME and THEFT.** Spain's crime rate has increased dramatically in the last several years, especially in the cities and some of the larger resorts. Muggings and petty theft are all too common these days, so it's only sensible to take certain precautions:

● Secure passport, traveller's cheques, credit cards and reserves of cash in a money belt or, better still, entrust valuables to hotel safe-deposit boxes. A shoulder bag worn bandolier-style may discourage pickpockets and bag snatchers.

● Dress modestly and forswear jewellery—especially gold chains.

● Lock your car and stow any possessions out of sight in the boot (trunk).

● Never leave anything of value on the front or back seat or rear shelf while driving, above all in Sevilla. Enterprising thieves have been known to smash the window with a rock and make off while the driver was idling at a red light.

● Don't offer resistance should you be attacked. Some thieves are armed with knives and they might just use them.

Certain areas frequented by tourists are a target for thieves—the foot-path up to Gibralfaro in Málaga, for example, and the area around the castle. Inquire before you set out alone—especially at night. While a few tourists to the Costa del Sol have been the victims of violence, the great majority who follow the above recommendations enjoy carefree holidays.

I want to report a theft.          **Ha habido un robo.**


**D** **DRIVING IN SPAIN**

**Entering Spain:** To bring your car into Spain you should have:

| International Driving Permit, or a legalized and certified translation of your home licence | Car registration papers | Green Card (an extension to your regular insurance policy, making it valid for foreign countries) |
| --- | --- | --- |

*Also recommended:* With your certificate of insurance, you should carry a bail bond. If you injure somebody in an accident in Spain, you can be imprisoned while the accident is under investigation. This bond will bail you out. Apply to your automobile association or insurance company.

A nationality sticker must be prominently displayed on the back of your car. The use of seat belts is obligatory; fines for non-compliance are stiff. A red reflecting warning triangle is compulsory when driving on motorways (expressways). Motorcycle riders and their passengers must wear crash helmets.

**Driving conditions:** Drive on the right. Pass on the left. Yield right of way to all traffic coming from the right. Spanish drivers tend to use their horn when overtaking (passing).

Main roads are adequate to very good and improving all the time. Secondary roads can be bumpy. The main danger of driving in Spain comes from impatience, especially on busy roads. A large percentage of accidents occur when passing, so take it easy. Wait until you have a long, unobstructed view.

Spanish truck and lorry drivers will often wave you on (by hand signal or by flashing their right directional signal) if it's clear ahead.

**Parking:** Many towns charge a token fee for parking during working hours; the cities more. The attendants are often disabled, and it's usual to round off the price of the ticket upwards.

It is forbidden to park the car facing oncoming traffic.

**Traffic police:** Spanish roads are probably the best patrolled in all Europe. The men who do the patrolling are the motorcycle police of the Civil Guard *(Guardia Civil)*. They always ride in pairs and are always armed. They are extremely courteous at helping you find your way, are efficient with minor mechanical problems and go out of their way to help you if you have a breakdown.

The most common offences include speeding, passing without flashing your lights, travelling too close to the car in front, and driving with a burned-out head- or rear-lamp. (Spanish law requires you to carry a set of spare bulbs at all times.)

**Fuel and oil:** Service stations, once sparsely dotted around the countryside, are now plentiful, particularly in tourist areas, but it's a good idea to keep an eye on the gauge in deserted areas.

## Fluid measures

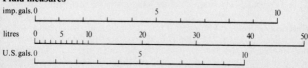

**D** **Breakdowns:** Spanish garages are as efficient as any, but in tourist areas major repairs may take several days because of the heavy workload. Spare parts are readily available for all major makes of cars.

**Road signs:** Most road signs employed in Spain are international. But there are some written signs you will come across, too:

| | |
|---|---|
| **Aduana** | Customs |
| **¡Alto!** | Halt! |
| **Aparcamiento** | Parking |
| **Autopista (de peaje)** | (Toll) motorway (expressway) |
| **Calzada deteriorada** | Bad road |
| **Calzada estrecha** | Narrow road |
| **Ceda el paso** | Give way (Yield) |
| **Cruce peligroso** | Dangerous crossroads |
| **Cuidado** | Caution |
| **Curva peligrosa** | Dangerous bend |
| **Despacio** | Slow |
| **Desviación** | Diversion (Detour) |
| **Escuela** | School |
| **Obras** | Road works (Men working) |
| **¡Pare!** | Stop! |
| **Peligro** | Danger |
| **Prohibido adelantar** | No overtaking (passing) |
| **Prohibido aparcar** | No parking |
| **Puesto de socorro** | First-aid post |
| **Salida de camiones** | Lorry (Truck) exit |

| | |
|---|---|
| (International) Driving Licence | **carné de conducir (internacional)** |
| car registration papers | **permiso de circulación** |
| Green Card | **carta verde** |
| Can I park here? | **¿Se puede aparcar aquí?** |
| Are we on the right road for...? | **¿Es ésta la carretera hacia...?** |
| Full tank, please, top grade. | **Llénelo, por favor, con super.** |
| Check the oil/tires/battery. | **Por favor, controle el aceite/los neumáticos/la batería.** |
| I've had a breakdown. | **Mi coche se ha estropeado.** |
| There's been an accident. | **Ha habido un accidente.** |

**Entering Gibraltar:** You must be in possession of the Green Card to visit Gibraltar by car, which means that tourists driving hired cars may not ride across the border. They can, however, park on the Spanish side, cross on foot and take a taxi on the other side.

**DRUGS.** Until the 1980s, Spain had one of the strictest drug laws in Europe. Then possession of small quantities for personal use was legalized. Now the pendulum has swung back in the other direction: possession and sale of drugs is once again a criminal offense in Spain.

**ELECTRIC CURRENT** *(corriente eléctrica).* 220-volt A.C. is becoming standard, but older installations of 125 volts can still be found. Check before plugging in. If the voltage is 125, American appliances (e.g. razors) built for 60 cycles will run on 50-cycle European current, but more slowly.

| | |
|---|---|
| What's the voltage—125 or 220? | **¿Cuál es el voltaje—ciento veinticinco (125) o doscientos veinte (220)?** |
| an adaptor/a battery | **un adaptador/una pila** |

**EMERGENCIES** *(urgencia).* Being completely familiar with local conditions, your hotel desk-clerk or a taxi driver can be of great help.

**Emergency telephone numbers:**

| | Fire | First Aid | Police |
|---|---|---|---|
| Fuengirola | 47 31 57 | 47 31 57 | 091 |
| Málaga | 30 60 60 | 29 03 40 | 091 |
| Marbella | 77 43 49 | 77 27 49 | 091 |
| Torremolinos | 38 39 39 | 38 16 86 | 091 |

Depending on the nature of the emergency, refer to the separate entries in this section such as CONSULATES, MEDICAL CARE, POLICE, etc.

Though we hope you'll never need them, here are a few key words you might like to learn in advance:

| | | | |
|---|---|---|---|
| Careful | **Cuidado** | Police | **Policía** |
| Fire | **Fuego** | Stop | **Deténgase** |
| Help | **Socorro** | Stop thief | **Al ladrón** |

**ENTRY FORMALITIES and CUSTOMS CONTROLS.** Most visitors require only a valid passport to enter Spain.

**E**　　Here's what you can carry into Spain duty-free and, upon your return home, into your own country:

| Into: | Cigarettes | | Cigars | | Tobacco | Spirits | Wine |
|---|---|---|---|---|---|---|---|
| Spain 1) | 300 | or | 75 | or | 350 g. | 1.5 l. and 5 l. | |
| 2) | 200 | or | 50 | or | 250 g. | 1 l. or 2 l. | |
| Australia | 200 | or | 250 g. | or | 250 g. | 1 l. or 1 l. | |
| Canada | 200 | and | 50 | and | 900 g. | 1.1 l. or 1.1 l. | |
| Eire | 200 | or | 50 | or | 250 g. | 1 l. and 2 l. | |
| N. Zealand | 200 | or | 50 | or | 250 g. | 1.1 l. and 4.5 l. | |
| S. Africa | 400 | and | 50 | and | 250 g. | 1 l. and 2 l. | |
| U.K. | 200 | or | 50 | or | 250 g. | 1 l. and 2 l. | |
| U.S.A. | 200 | and | 100 | and | 3) | 1 l. or 1 l. | |

1) Visitors arriving from EEC countries.
2) Visitors arriving from other countries.
3) A reasonable quantity.

**Currency restrictions.** Tourists may bring an unlimited amount of Spanish or foreign currency into the country. Departing, though, you must declare any amount beyond the equivalent of 500,000 pesetas. Thus if you plan to carry large sums in and out again it's wise to declare your currency on arrival as well as on departure.

| | |
|---|---|
| I've nothing to declare. | **No tengo nada que declarar.** |
| It's for my personal use. | **Es para mi uso personal.** |

**F**　**FIRE** *(incendio)*. Forest fires are a real menace in hot, dry Andalusia, so be very careful where you throw your cigarette butts. If you are camping, make sure your fire is extinguished before you move on.

**G**　**GUIDES and INTERPRETERS.** Apply to the Edificio Salome at: Carretera de Benalmádena, 4, Torremolinos; tel. 38 60 42.

| | |
|---|---|
| We'd like an English-speaking guide. | **Queremos un guía que hable inglés.** |
| I need an English interpreter. | **Necesito un intérprete de inglés.** |

**HAIRDRESSERS\***. Most large hotels have their own salons and the standard is generally very high. Men's barbers are called *barbería,* women's salons, *peluquería.* Prices are far lower in neighbourhood salons in the towns than in the resorts and chic hotels. See also TIPPING.

The following vocabulary will help:

| | |
|---|---|
| I'd like a shampoo and set. | **Quiero lavado y marcado.** |
| I want a... | **Quiero...** |
| haircut | **un corte de pelo** |
| razor cut | **un corte a navaja** |
| blow-dry (brushing) | **un modelado** |
| permanent wave | **una permanente** |
| colour rinse/hair-dye | **un reflejo/un tinte** |
| manicure | **una manicura** |
| Don't cut it too short. | **No me lo corte mucho.** |
| A little more off (here). | **Un poco más (aquí).** |

**HOTELS and ACCOMMODATION\*** *(hotel; alojamiento).* Spanish hotel prices are no longer government-controlled. Before the guest takes the room he fills out a form indicating the hotel category, room number and price and signs it. Breakfast is generally included in the room rate.

**Other forms of accommodation:**

**Hostal:** Modest hotels, often family concerns, graded by stars (one to three). Rates overlap with the lower range of hotels, e.g. a three-star *hostal* usually costs about the same as a two-star hotel.

**Pensión:** Boarding houses, graded one to three, with few amenities.

**Fonda:** Village inns, clean and unpretentious.

**Parador:** Of special interest to motorists, since usually located outside towns, often in very old or historic buildings. State-run. Advance booking essential.

**Albergue:** Wayside inns; stay generally limited to two nights. Also state-run.

**H** **Refugio:** Mountain hunting lodges.

**Residencia:** When referred to as *hostal-residencia* or *hotel-residencia*, this term indicates a hotel without a restaurant.

| a single/double room | **una habitación sencilla/doble** |
|---|---|
| with bath/shower | **con baño/ducha** |

What's the rate per night?   **¿Cuál es el precio por noche?**

**L** **LANGUAGE.** The national language of Spain, Castilian Spanish, is spoken throughout the Costa del Sol area. Even if you learned Spanish at school, you might find the local accent a little difficult to understand at first. English is widely spoken in the resort towns.

| Good morning/Good day | **Buenos días** |
|---|---|
| Good afternoon/Good evening | **Buenas tardes** |
| Good night | **Buenas noches** |
| Please | **Por favor** |
| Thank you | **Gracias** |
| You're welcome | **De nada** |
| Goodbye | **Adiós** |

The Berlitz phrase book, SPANISH FOR TRAVELLERS, covers most situations you are likely to encounter in your travels in Spain. The Berlitz Spanish-English/English-Spanish pocket dictionary contains some 12,500 concepts, plus a menu-reader supplement.

| Do you speak English? | **¿Habla usted inglés?** |
|---|---|
| I don't speak Spanish. | **No hablo español.** |

**LAUNDRY and DRY-CLEANING.** Most hotels will handle laundry and dry-cleaning, but they'll usually charge more than a laundry *(lavandería)* or a dry-cleaners *(tintorería)*. For still greater savings, you can try a do-it-yourself launderette *(launderama)*.

| Where's the nearest | **¿Dónde está la lavandería/** |
|---|---|
| laundry/dry-cleaners? | **tintorería más cercana?** |
| I want these clothes | **Quiero que limpien/laven** |
| cleaned/washed. | **esta ropa.** |
| When will it be ready? | **¿Cuándo estará lista?** |
| I must have this for | **La necesito para mañana por** |
| tomorrow morning. | **la mañana.** |

**LOST PROPERTY.** The first thing to do when you discover you've lost something is obviously to retrace your steps. If nothing comes to light, report the loss to the Municipal Police or the Guardia Civil.

I've lost my wallet/handbag/ passport.

**He perdido mi cartera/bolso/ pasaporte.**

**MAPS.** The Spanish National Tourist Office issues excellent free maps of major towns, resorts and tourist regions, with places of interest to visitors clearly marked. Firestone publishes an up-to-date map of the Costa del Sol (Castell de Ferro to Tarifa), while Michelin's plan of Andalusia covers the entire region.

The maps in this guide were prepared by Falk-Verlag, Hamburg.

a street plan of...
a road map of this region

**un plano de la ciudad de...**
**un mapa de carreteras de esta comarca**

**MEDICAL CARE.** By far the best solution, to be completely at ease, is to take out a special health insurance policy to cover the risk of illness and accident while on holiday. Your travel agent can also fix you up with Spanish tourist insurance (ASTES), but it is a slow-moving process. ASTES covers doctors' fees and clinical care.

Health care in the resort areas and in the major cities is good. Most of the major resort towns have private clinics; the cities and rural areas are served by municipal or provincial hospitals.

For minor ailments, visit the local first-aid post *(ambulatorio).* Away from your hotel, don't hesitate to ask the police or a tourist information office for help. At your hotel, ask the staff to help you.

*Farmacias* (chemists' shops, drugstores) are usually open during normal shopping hours. After hours, at least one per town remains open all night, called *farmacia de guardia,* and its location is posted in the window of all other *farmacias.*

Where's the nearest (all-night) pharmacy?
I need a doctor/dentist.
I've a pain here.

sunburn
sunstroke
an upset stomach
insect bite

**¿Dónde está la farmacia (de guardia) más cercana?**
**Necesito un médico/dentista.**
**Me duele aquí.**

**quemadura del sol**
**una insolación**
**molestias de estómago**
**una picadura de insecto**

117

**M** **MEETING PEOPLE.** The Spanish, as a whole, are one of the world's most open and hospitable people, easy to talk to and approach, generous to a fault.

The *andaluz* (Andalusian) is considered throughout the Spanish-speaking world one of the most witty and charming inhabitants of the peninsula. His way of speaking—rapid, staccato, with both *c* and *z* pronounced "s"—is quaint (though very imperious, to an outsider); the fiery, passionate temperament imputed to Spaniards is most pronounced in this region. The noise-level of conversations can be quite deafening over any length of time. But what you perhaps take for a quarrel is more often than not simply news and gossip being transmitted... passionately.

Spain's strict moral attitudes still apply in rural Andalusia, although tourism has loosened the rules. If a pretty local girl should smile at an admirer, it should not be taken as an invitation. Spanish men, on the contrary, consider all foreign women to be fair game.

## MONEY MATTERS

**Currency:** The monetary unit of Spain is the *peseta* (abbreviated *pta.*).
   Coins: 1, 2, 5, 10, 25, 50, 100, 200 pesetas.
   Banknotes: 100, 200, 500, 1,000, 2,000, 5,000, 10,000 pesetas.

A 5-peseta coin is traditionally called a *duro,* so if someone should quote a price as 10 duros, he means 50 pesetas. For currency restrictions, see ENTRY FORMALITIES AND CUSTOMS CONTROLS.

**Banking hours** are from 9 a.m. to 2 p.m. Monday to Friday, also till 1 p.m. on Saturdays in June, July and August.

Banks are closed on Sundays and holidays—watch out, too, for those obscure holidays which always seem to crop up in Spain! Outside normal banking hours, many travel agencies and other businesses displaying a *cambio* sign will change foreign currency into pesetas. The exchange rate is a bit less favourable than in the banks. Both banks and exchange offices pay slightly more for traveller's cheques than for cash. Always take your passport with you when you go to exchange money.

**Credit cards:** All the internationally recognized cards are accepted by hotels, restaurants and businesses in Spain.

**Eurocheques:** You'll have no problem settling bills or paying for
118 purchases with Eurocheques.

**Traveller's cheques:** In tourist areas, shops and all banks, hotels and travel agencies accept them, though you're likely to get a better exchange rate at a national or regional bank. Remember always to take your passport with you if you expect to cash a traveller's cheque. Only cash small amounts at a time, and keep the balance of your cheques in the hotel safe if possible. At the very least, be sure to keep your receipt and a list of the serial numbers of the cheques in a separate place to facilitate a refund in case of loss or theft.

**Paying cash:** Although many shops and bars will accept payment in sterling or dollars, you're better off paying in pesetas. Shops will invariably give you less than the bank rate for foreign currency.

**Prices:** Although Spain has by no means escaped the scourge of inflation, the Costa del Sol remains quite competitive with the other tourist capitals of Europe. An exciting night on the town—either at a discotheque or a flamenco nightclub—can be had for a reasonable amount by North-European and American standards. In the realm of eating, drinking and smoking, Spain still provides indisputable value for money.

Certain rates are listed on page 103 to give you an idea of what things cost.

| | |
|---|---|
| Where's the nearest bank/currency exchange office? | **¿Dónde está el banco/la oficina de cambio más cercana?** |
| I want to change some pounds/dollars. | **Quiero cambiar libras/dólares.** |
| Do you accept traveller's cheques? | **¿Acepta usted cheques de viaje?** |
| Can I pay with this credit card? | **¿Puedo pagar con esta tarjeta de crédito?** |
| How much is that? | **¿Cuánto es?** |

**NEWSPAPERS and MAGAZINES** (*periódico; revista*). In major tourist areas you can buy most European and British newspapers and magazines on the day of publication. U.S. magazines are available, as well as the Paris-based *International Herald Tribune*.

On the Costa del Sol an English-language newspaper, the *Iberian Daily Sun*, is available. A monthly publication, *Lookout*, describing itself as "The Magazine about Spain", is a good window on the country.

| | |
|---|---|
| Have you any English-language newspapers? | **¿Tienen periódicos en inglés?** |

**P** **PHOTOGRAPHY** (*fotografía*). For the knowledgeable amateur or professional photographer Spain is a bonanza of picture opportunities. It is no less so for the once-a-year holiday shutter-bug, but for him Spain—and particularly southern Spain—can present a photographic problem. All those white-walled villages and sparkling seas, potentially marvellous holiday snaps, fool the electronic eyes on automatic cameras, tending to darken pictures. Read your camera instruction book in advance, or have a chat with a camera dealer and show him your equipment.

All popular film makes and sizes are available in Spain. Prices are generally higher than in the rest of Europe or North America, so it is advisable to bring a good stock.

Photo shops in major resorts can develop and print black and white or colour film in 24 to 48 hours at reasonable prices, and some specialize in 1-hour service.

The Spanish films, *Negra* and *Valca* in black and white, and *Negracolor* in colour, are of good quality and cheaper than the internationally known brands.

| | |
|---|---|
| I'd like some film for this camera. | **Quisiera un carrete para esta máquina.** |
| black and white film | **carrete en blanco y negro** |
| for colour prints | **carrete para película en color** |
| colour-slide film | **carrete de diapositivas** |
| 35-mm film | **carrete treinta y cinco** |
| super-8 | **super ocho** |
| How long will it take to develop (and print) this? | **¿Cuánto tardará en revelar (y sacar copias de) este carrete?** |
| May I take a picture? | **¿Puedo sacar una foto?** |

**POLICE** (*policía*). There are three police forces in Spain: the *Policía Municipal*, who are attached to the local town hall and usually wear a blue uniform; the *Cuerpo Nacional de Policía*, a national anti-crime unit recognized by their blue-and-white uniforms; and the *Guardia Civil*, the national police force patrol highways as well as towns.

If you need police assistance, you can call on any one of the three. Spanish police are efficient, strict and particularly courteous to foreign visitors.

| | |
|---|---|
| Where's the nearest police station? | **¿Dónde está la comisaría más cercana?** |

## PUBLIC HOLIDAYS *(fiesta)*

| | | |
|---|---|---|
| January 1 | *Año Nuevo* | New Year's Day |
| January 6 | *Epifanía* | Epiphany |
| March 19 | *San José* | St. Joseph's Day |
| May 1 | *Día del Trabajo* | Labour Day |
| July 25 | *Santiago Apóstol* | St. James's Day |
| August 15 | *Asunción* | Assumption |
| October 12 | *Día de la Hispanidad* | Discovery of America Day (Columbus Day) |
| November 1 | *Todos los Santos* | All Saints' Day |
| December 6 | *Día de la Constitución Española* | Constitution Day |
| December 25 | *Navidad* | Christmas Day |
| Movable dates: | *Jueves Santo* | Maundy Thursday |
| | *Viernes Santo* | Good Friday |
| | *Lunes de Pascua* | Easter Monday (Catalonia only) |
| | *Corpus Christi* | Corpus Christi |
| | *Inmaculada Concepción* | Immaculate Conception (normally December 8) |

In Spain there are many regional public holidays, including Andalucía Day *(Día de Andalucía),* celebrated along the coast.

**RADIO and TV** *(radio; televisión).* Broadcasts in English can be picked up from Gibraltar, as can French-language broadcasts from Morocco. Reception at night is usually good enough to allow listeners to tune in to most European countries on medium-wave transistor portables, including the BBC World Service and the Voice of America. National television programmes are all in Spanish, but it is possible to receive English-language broadcasts from Gibraltar between Fuengirola and Sotogrande.

**RELIGIOUS SERVICES.** The national religion of Spain is Roman Catholic. Mass and services in English are conducted in Benalmádena-Costa (Catholic and Protestant), Fuengirola (Protestant), Málaga

**R** (Catholic, Protestant and Jewish), Torremolinos (Catholic and Protestant). For further details, refer to *Lookout* magazine.

**S** **SIESTA.** Siesta means a nap, and what it boils down to is a four-hour lunch break. Although this custom seems to be dying out in some areas of northern Spain, it is still observed on the Costa del Sol and in Andalusia. Shops generally close from 1 or 2 to 4 or 5 p.m. and then stay open till 7.30 (many close much later).

**T** **TIME DIFFERENCES.** Spanish time coincides with most of Western Europe—Greenwich Mean Time plus one hour. In summer, another hour is added for Daylight Saving Time (Summer Time).

Summer Time chart:

| New York | London | **Spain** | Jo'burg | Sydney | Auckland |
|----------|--------|-----------|---------|--------|----------|
| 6 a.m. | 11 a.m. | **noon** | noon | 8 p.m. | 10 p.m. |

What time is it?                    **¿Qué hora es?**

**TIPPING.** Since a service charge is normally included in hotel and restaurant bills, tipping is not obligatory. However, it's appropriate to tip bellboys, filling-station attendants, bullfight ushers, etc., for their service. The chart below gives some suggestions as to what to leave.

| Porter, per bag | minimum 50 ptas. |
|-----------------|------------------|
| Maid, for extra services | 100–200 ptas. |
| Lavatory attendant | 25–50 ptas. |
| Waiter | 10% (optional) |
| Taxi driver | 10% |
| Hairdresser/Barber | 10% |
| Tour guide | 10% |

**TOILETS.** There are many expressions for "toilets" in Spanish: *aseos*, *servicios*, *W.C.*, *water* and *retretes*. The first two are more common.

122      Public toilets are to be found in most large Spanish towns, but rarely in villages. However, just about every bar and restaurant has a toilet

available for public use. It's considered polite to buy a coffee or a glass of wine if you drop in specifically to use the conveniences.

Where are the toilets?          **¿Dónde están los servicios?**

**TOURIST INFORMATION OFFICES** *(oficina de turismo).* Information about Costa del Sol may be obtained from Spanish National Tourist Offices, maintained in many countries.

**Canada:** 60 Bloor St. West, Suite 201, Toronto, Ont. M4W-3B8; tel.: (416) 961-3131

**United Kingdom:** 57, St. James's St., London SW1 A1LD; tel.: (01) 499-0901.

**U.S.A.:** 845 N. Michigan Ave., Chicago, IL 60611; tel.: (312) 944-0215.

4800 The Galleria, 5085 Westheimer Road, Houston, TX 77056; tel.: (713) 8407411.

8383 Wilshire Boulevard, Suite 960, Beverly Hills, Los Angeles, CA 90211; tel.: (213) 658-7188/93.

665 5th Ave., New York, NY 10022; tel.: (212) 759-8822.

Casa del Hidalgo, Hypolita & St. George Streets, St. Augustine, FL 31084; tel.: (904) 829-6460.

These offices will supply you with a wide range of colourful and informative brochures and maps in English on the various towns and regions in Spain. They will also let you consult a copy of the master directory of hotels on the coast, listing all facilities and prices.

On the spot there are official tourist information offices which normally are open from 9 a.m. to 1 p.m. and from 4 to 7 p.m. At all offices, somebody will be able to give advice and suggestions in English.

| | |
|---|---|
| **Airport:** | tel. 31 20 44. |
| **Benalmádena-Costa:** | Carretera de Cádiz (near Hotel Alay); tel. 44 13 63. |
| **Fuengirola:** | Avenida Condes de San Isidro; tel. 47 61 66. |
| **Málaga:** | Marqués de Larios, 5; tel. 21 34 45. |
| **Marbella:** | Miguel Cano, 1; tel. 77 14 42. |
| **Ronda:** | Plaza de España, 1; tel. 87 12 72. |
| **Torremolinos:** | Calle Guetaria; tel. 38 15 78. |

Where is the tourist office?          **¿Dónde está la oficina de turismo?**

# T TRANSPORT

**Boats:** Málaga is port of call, as well as departure point, for a variety of cruise ships and ferries, serving destinations as distant as Sydney and Cape Town as well as many major Mediterranean ports (Genoa, Tangiers, Melilla, Marseilles). Cars can be taken aboard the ferries. From Algeciras, other boats leave for Ceuta and Tangiers.

**Bus services** *(servicio de autobús)*: The Costa del Sol and the major towns of inland Andalusia are well served by several private bus companies. Destinations are clearly marked on the front of the bus.

Buses are cheaper than trains, and a two-way bus ticket will be less expensive than a travel-agency tour.

Information on schedules and fares can be obtained from tourist information offices in the coastal resort towns or from the central bus station *(estación central de autobuses)* in larger towns.

**Taxis*** *(taxi)*: Málaga taxis have meters, but in villages along the rest of the coast they usually don't, so it's a good idea to check the fare before you get in. If you take a long trip—for example between two villages—you will be charged a two-way fare whether you make the return journey or not.

In Málaga the fare is a basic rate, with an additional charge per kilometre. Large pieces of luggage will cost extra.

All taxis carry price lists in several languages. These lists have been approved by the authorities. If you feel you've been overcharged, you can always ask the driver to show you the list.

By Spanish law taxis may only take four persons per vehicle (although some are willing to risk a fifth if it is a baby or child).

A green light and/or a *Libre* ("free") sign indicates a taxi is available.

You can also call for a cab:

Estepona, tel. 80 12 97.
Fuengirola, tel. 47 20 30/47 50 41.
Málaga, tel. 22 31 07/32 79 50.
Marbella, tel. 77 00 53.
Torremolinos, tel. 38 10 30/38 21 52.

**Trains** *(tren):* While local trains are very slow, stopping at almost all stations, long-distance services, especially the *Talgo* and *Ter,* are fast and reasonably punctual. First-class coaches are comfortable; second-class, adequate. Tickets can be purchased at travel agencies as well as at railway stations *(estación de ferrocarril)*.

| | |
|---|---|
| *Talgo, Intercity, Electrotren, Ter, Tren Estrella* | Luxury diesel, first and second classes; supplementary charge over regular fare |
| *Expreso, Rápido* | Long-distance expresses, stopping at main stations only; supplementary charge |
| *Omnibus, Tranvía, Automotor* | Local trains, with frequent stops, usually second class only |
| *Auto Expreso* | Car train |
| *coche cama* | Sleeping-car with 1-, 2- or 3-bed compartments, washing facilities |
| *coche comedor* | Dining-car |
| *litera* | Sleeping-berth car *(couchette)* with blankets, sheets and pillows |

From Málaga, it's a simple matter to go along the coast to the main resorts. Local trains leave each half-hour, from 7 a.m. to 11 p.m. (in both directions), between Málaga, Torremolinos, Arroyo de la Miel, Los Boliches and Fuengirola. The whole journey takes some 45 minutes.

The mainline RENFE station in Malaga is in:

Calle Cuarteles; tel. 31 25 00.

For information and tickets, apply to:

Calle Strachan, 2; tel. 21 31 22.

| | |
|---|---|
| Where is the (nearest) bus stop? | **¿Dónde está la parada de autobuses (más cercana)?** |
| When's the next bus/boat for…? | **¿A qué hora sale el próximo autobús/barco para…?** |
| I want a ticket to… | **Quiero un billete para…** |
| single (one-way) | **ida** |
| return (round-trip) | **ida y vuelta** |
| Will you tell me when to get off? | **¿Podría indicarme cuándo tengo que bajar?** |
| Where can I get a taxi? | **¿Dónde puedo coger un taxi?** |
| What's the fare to…? | **¿Cuánto es la tarifa a…?** |

**W** **WATER.** If you're particularly sensitive to a change in water, you may want to order the bottled variety. Both still (non-carbonated) and fizzy (carbonated) water are available.

| | |
|---|---|
| a bottle of mineral water | **una botella de agua mineral** |
| fizzy | **con gas** |
| still | **sin gas** |
| Is this drinking water? | **¿El agua es potable?** |

**Y** **YOUTH HOSTELS** *(albergue de juventud)*. Youth hostels do exist in Spain, but are few and far between. Note that the Spanish word *hostal* does not mean "youth hostel", but a certain type of hotel.

---

## SOME USEFUL EXPRESSIONS

| | |
|---|---|
| yes/no | **sí/no** |
| please/thank you | **por favor/gracias** |
| excuse me/you're welcome | **perdone/de nada** |
| where/when/how | **dónde/cuándo/cómo** |
| how long/how far | **cuánto tiempo/a qué distancia** |
| yesterday/today/tomorrow | **ayer/hoy/mañana** |
| day/week/month/year | **día/semana/mes/año** |
| left/right | **izquierda/derecha** |
| up/town | **arriba/abajo** |
| good/bad | **bueno/malo** |
| big/small | **grande/pequeño** |
| cheap/expensive | **barato/caro** |
| hot/cold | **caliente/frío** |
| old/new | **viejo/nuevo** |
| open/closed | **abierto/cerrado** |
| here/there | **aquí/allí** |
| free (vacant)/occupied | **libre/ocupado** |
| early/late | **temprano/tarde** |
| What does this mean? | **¿Qué quiere decir esto?** |
| I don't understand. | **No comprendo.** |
| Waiter!/Waitress! | **¡Camarero!/¡Camarera!** |

126

# Index

An asterix (*) next to a page number indicates a map reference. Where there is more than one set of page references, the one in bold type refers to the main entry. For the index to Practical Information, see inside front cover.